USE your Power!

Louis

SERVICE
IS A
SUPERPOWER

www.mascotbooks.com

For more information, please contact:
Mascot Books
620 Herndon Parkway #320
Herndon, VA 20170
info@mascotbooks.com

Library of Congress Control Number: 2019916016

CPSIA Code: PRFRE0120A
ISBN-13: 978-1-64543-264-7

Printed in Canada

"To Barbara Epstein, who made virtually all of this possible."

SERVICE
IS A
SUPERPOWER

Lessons Learned in a **Magic Kingdom**

LOUIE GRAVANCE

CONTENTS

INTRODUCTION

S ervice is a superpower.

The more I teach this, the more I learn it. Countless books and missives have been written about customer service and its potential effects on a company's bottom line. Rarely, however, do we explore the effects the delivery of service-excellence has on the person providing it. Is there a benefit to the service employee for exceeding expectations beyond just managing to keep a job? I've come to know that there is. In fact, I'm living proof of it.

You also know this to be true, or you wouldn't have gravitated to this book or bother to read it. My guess is you already know there is power in service but haven't figured out a way to consistently turn it to your own advantage.

It pains me when I witness bad service at a store, restaurant, or hospital, and not only for the obvious reasons. It bothers me because it's a waste, a missed opportunity. Much like watching someone holding a magic wand in their hand only to toss it to the ground because they didn't perceive its worth or understand how to use it. (More on magic wands later, a lot more.)

Every person holding this book has made an impact on someone else's life through service and forgotten all about it. The receiver hasn't forgotten, but you have. Don't feel bad; we have all forgotten at some point, if not always. You have failed to remember—I guarantee it.

Magical moments in service do not just happen at theme parks. They happen everywhere, and you are probably not aware of being responsible for hundreds of moments or how they've impacted your life. This book intends to explore this magic and provide the reader a method for making it happen consistently.

It is my sincere hope that by developing the Ten Skills of the Service Superhero, you will come to understand and utilize what I have known for years:

GREAT SERVICE SERVES THE SERVER FIRST!

This book is in two parts. Part one explains my path to discovering the impact and power of delivering service-excellence, and I'll explain the lessons learned in a magic kingdom. Part two applies those lessons so that you, the reader, can develop the "ten skills of the service superhero" and drive your own work "narrative" to ultimate success.

We'll begin by setting the context through my own experience, which led me on a journey from the farmlands of Central California, past the tinsel of Hollywood, to a massive magic kingdom and beyond. However, the bulk of this endeavor deals with honing the power and force of customer service. (An unseen force not terribly different than the one Luke Skywalker uses to raise a spacecraft, seemingly with only his concentration and facial muscles.)

I do a lot of talking. A whole lot. However, I'm not one of those people who will make your flight from New York to California miserable with chatter; nor am I someone who starts up conversations with total strangers while waiting at the supermarket checkout. However, I do speak for a *living*. Fortunately for me, since it's one of the few premiere skills I possess, talking can be lucrative.

"But what could you possibly talk about that people would pay you for?" my father would ask quizzically. While not exactly Zig Ziglar or Tony Robbins (yet), I do well enough to have inspired a raised eyebrow from Dad.

"Well, Dad," I offered, "I share what I've learned from designing and delivering service training for leading brands like Disney to help other companies and people reach greatness in customer service." I'm not sure he bought my elevator pitch, but what I described to him is exactly my purpose, primarily through humorous keynote speeches at corporate events but also by taking occasional consulting projects or creating a training initiative from scratch.

Many of the leaders I have worked with have encouraged me to finally sit down and write something that captures the message of my talks and seminars. (My speaking agent has **implored** me to do it.) This encouragement has inspired me to work through my slight case of attention deficit and finally write down my methods.

To be clear: While much of my service philosophy has been influenced by my years at the Walt Disney Company, it is neither my intent nor my function to either compete with, or represent that company here. If you're interested in the specific tenets and systems of how Disney trains its "cast," I highly recommend calling the folks in the professional programs unit at the Disney Institute in Orlando, Florida.

Neither will there be any attempt in this book to hide the rather obvious metaphysical underpinnings of this message. While no religious dogma is presented in any way, we do reference the investment of spirit and emotion into one's job. The book *A Course in Miracles* ("a curriculum for those seeking to achieve spiritual transformation," transcribed in 1976) has had a profound influence on my life and frame of reference exhibited within these pages.

I want to reiterate: This is not a book on "The Disney Way" but, rather, how my experience with the Disney University, the Disney Institute, and a life in show business informed my thinking about how you can benefit from service-excellence. These are the same concepts and thinking processes that guided my efforts in reshaping the service culture at Bank of America, ING Financial, and many other companies.

There's a great chance that you work for a company that has had one customer service initiative after another, only to have them perceived as merely the "flavor of the month." Many of these efforts have probably worked for a short while before your team went back to "task thinking," and disengaging.

If you're an employer, frustrated by the service performance of your team, here's some rough news: It's not because they don't know *how*, it's because they don't know *why*. They simply don't grasp what's in it for them. No one has convinced them that service-excellence will always seek and find other excellence, no matter where.

"But we've made our expectations clear and communicated exactly what we need them to do," you may say. And you probably have. But have you told them what you need them to *be*? There can be a considerable difference between DOING something or BEING something.

In turn, if you're an individual providing a less-than superior customer experience, it is almost always an issue of **won't** or **don't** and very rarely about **can't**.

My life has been graced with an embarrassing amount of good fortune, and I'm very grateful to have learned all I've learned. To keep it, I need to share it. Virtually everything I've managed to be or achieve has come from serving someone or giving something up or away. This is because service really is a SUPERPOWER!

The more you teach this, the more you'll learn it too.

CHAPTER ONE
THERE'S NO BUSINESS BUT SHOW BUSINESS

The concept of "There's no business BUT show business" is a theme that underlies most of my presentations, and it comes from lessons well learned throughout a show business career that began when I was fourteen. (So, too, did my education in the science of creating "brand relationships" through imagery and suggestion, but that's another book.)

At the start of creating each new training program—developing a power-talk or planning a corporate culture-shift—I begin the process by remembering my first rule: **context over content.** Context acts as the **proscenium** that frames the "stage of your show" or personal narrative. This can't be stressed enough, and it is as true for an individual exactly as it is for an organization: Context helps us identify intent.

With this book, therefore, we'll begin with a quick trip through my curious and circuitous career path to set the context for how I learned what I learned and know what I know. Most anecdotes illustrate a concept that we'll use later in the book to frame your path to service-excellence.

I'M AFRAID WE'RE GOING TO HAVE TO SHAVE YOUR HANDS

As I watched the nice make-up artist take a disposable razor to my hands (a pink Lady-Schick, as I recall), it suddenly occurred to me that, at twenty-four years old, my days of playing juveniles on television were probably coming to an end. At only 5'3" and looking younger than my age, playing kids on stage and screen had been a good niche since producers preferred not to hire actual minors if they didn't have to. I'd already clocked ten years in show business prior to having my digits sheared that day, appearing in everything from horror films to singing in soft drink commercials.

I was born and raised in Hanford, California, a very small town in the central valley akin to the feel and vibe of the movie *American Graffiti*. With a population of only 13,000 and surrounded by farms and dairies, it was nearly as idyllic as the America seen in early TV sitcoms of the 1960s. We got movies at our local theaters at least three months after their release, and the tallest structure was a grain silo.

On my eighth birthday, my mother (twenty-six years old at the time) was diagnosed with terminal cancer with a poor prognosis. However, she has just turned eighty, having recently left the hospital in high-heels a week after hip replacement. That tells you pretty much all you need to know about her, except that, while everyone finds their mother to be beautiful, mine's a bona fide "looker" and always has been. Virtually every one of my friends' mothers and teachers remarked about this frequently as I was growing up.

My father (rest his soul) adored everything I had no skills or interest in whatsoever. Hunting, fishing, sports, and getting your clothes dirty for fun were all things I found perplexingly foreign. Still, he was initially more supportive than others of my aptitude for "artistic endeavors" and enabled my early entry to the world of theater.

My first dream was to be either an "Imagineer" designing rides for Disneyland or animating cartoons at what was then known as WED (Walter Elias Disney) Enterprises. But something told me early on that, while having some talent as a draftsman, I would never be good enough to work for Disney. That dream would have to wait. Acting skills came a lot more easily and naturally to me, and life tilted me towards performing as a path of least resistance. Early and easy success eased my parents' initial reservations about a career in show business; therefore, I was allowed to move to Hollywood while still a minor.

Commercials were not only my bread and butter but also where I first began to understand the marriage between show business and commerce. A language all its own was spoken on those soundstages, and learning to use and be comfortable with this lexicon may be one of the reasons working in a culture like Disney came so easily to me later. We used to have a placard in the classrooms of Disney University that read: "Do You Speak Disney?" Oh, I certainly did, fluently. Is there any finer combination of "corporate" and "entertainment" than a Disney theme park?

Landing roles in any form of show business is a fiercely competitive racket, and the commercial world was no different. There is a unique skill set required for being a successful commercial actor. Timing, while always important in any kind of performance, is especially crucial in this world. Commercials are mapped out in sequences lasting fractions of a second, often requiring rapid-fire enunciation.

This is one of the reasons one tends to see many of the same actors hawking all different sorts of products; people who show a skill for the medium get hired over and over, often by the same ad agencies or directors. This was definitely true in my experience. Getting the first job was the toughest. Musical commercials were kind of my specialty, but before long, my family could see me on television selling everything from fried shrimp to Chryslers.

It was a commercial for Mattel Toys I was shooting on what was to be my "day of reckoning." Three other young men were also in the spot, all of us pretending to be fifteen years old. The ad featured one of the toy industry's very first hand-held computer toys, and its creators were extremely proud.

This particular day of shooting seemed to proceed like any other, except for there being even more "suits" on the set than usual due to the high cost and profile of the new marketing campaign. The four of us young men ran and jumped around a playground while excitedly squealing about this toy.

At the break for lunch I heard, "Hey Louie, can we speak to you for a second?" It was the director of the commercial, and he looked worried—never a good sign.

"Um, you see, uh," he stammered. "I'm afraid we're going to have to … have to … shave your hands." I must have looked astonished as he continued, "See, you look like all the other boys until we get to the product shot where we get to see your hands. Suddenly, you all throw your hands into frame, and it looks like three kids and a Hobbit put their hands on the toy. So, we gotta shave yours."

The other actors looked at me with a mixture of pity and scorn, much like the way dancers must look at a ballerina after she has just been told she's too old to do *Swan Lake* anymore.

Age-shamed at twenty-four!

Hence, the pink Lady-Schick and the moment I realized things were about to change in my career. A big change was in order.

Little did I know at the time that the change I anticipated was, in fact, to become a waiter. Now, I know this is the opposite trajectory a professional actor typically takes. Usually, one waits tables and *then* becomes a successful thespian. Luckily, that was not to be my "narrative."

It had been a good run of being an in-demand actor who specialized in playing kids, and I was grateful. The experience had taught me (more than I could appreciate at that young age) about creating and maintaining brands and the way emotional connections were made between product and consumer. I had discovered that every transaction is an emotional one, often grounded in a relationship that began with a commercial.

HOW WOULD YOU LIKE YOUR STEAK COOKED?

It turned out that I was correct: My days as a professional overage child had come to an end. I made a feeble attempt to be cool and hip by doing what a lot of guys my age were doing in the early '80s, namely shaving off hair, piercing an ear, wearing dark eye-liner, and trying to look as pale as possible. In short, youthful ridiculousness.

When going into the bank to cash what was to be my last big residual check, the bank teller took one look at me and earnestly asked, "What are you angry about?" The question was like a cold shower.

I wasn't *angry;* I was foolish. A realization came over me that, at twenty-four years old, I'd never played an adult onstage …

more significantly, though, the truth was I hadn't played one *offstage* either.

One of the things I am most grateful for in my life is that I was lucky enough to have that moment of clarity and the willingness to adopt the humility necessary to affect a profound personality change. It was like those scenes in movies when a hysterical character gets a swift slap to calm down and see straight. Not all of my teenage-playing colleagues had this epiphany, I'm sorry to say. Many became and continued to be confused and bitter by being an actor with the specialty of "youth."

Professional actors exist in a bubble that is very self-contained, self-centered and insular. How can an actor successfully portray a real person when they don't really know any? My life had revolved around "show folk" since I was fifteen, and I found myself profoundly ignorant about the way the rest of the world behaved.

Now, most actors wait tables or hustle other jobs before finally winding up on television, in a theatrical company, or in movies. I was lucky to have initial success in each one of those arenas and THEN wound up serving steak and seafood. A life path in reverse. Or so my immaturity informed me at the time. Actually, it was one of the most fortunate things that ever happened to me, before or after.

Stuart Anderson's Black Angus Steakhouse was a chain of massive restaurants with large bars and dance floors. Excellent quality for a chain in their price point, each location had as many as one hundred hardworking employees. How I managed to find a job at a restaurant in L.A. where I was the only person in show business I'll never know. Amidst that entire crew, nobody else had dreams or aspirations of winning an Oscar or even being a celebrity contestant on *The Match Game*, not one. I was finally among "real" people and it was like starting school again. There was only one rub: I had absolutely no idea how to wait tables. At all.

In fact, I had no experience or skill at serving food in any context. Immediately I realized that I had jumped into the deep end before learning how to swim. (Something I literally did at eight years old.) "What am I gonna do now?" I worried.

I didn't know exactly how to wait tables, but I was an actor, so I thought I could at least *act* like a gracious server until I gained the necessary skills. Then, it came to me … DISNEYLAND!

The most gracious service I had ever experienced was at Disneyland, a place that had been the object of my fascination since my earliest memory—the way the employees stood, the way they smiled, the way they *acted*. At the steakhouse, I decided to literally pretend like I worked at Disneyland, using good manners like a weapon for survival.

And you know what? It worked.

Because I conducted myself as if I worked for "The Happiest Place on Earth," people responded to me in kind, giving me the benefit of the doubt when their steak took twice as long as it should have to come out. This bought me time to develop serving skills while keeping my customers happy. Before long, I obtained the skills necessary to be something I never thought I'd be—an excellent waiter.

After two years, I was made head server and was almost as proud of that as any achievement I'd enjoyed being an actor. Frankly, in many ways, it felt like a much more honest way to make a living.

One day, I walked up to a table to take an order and, seated in the booth, was a director I had worked for several times on

TV. He looked at me with a degree of pity when I asked, "How would you like your steak cooked this evening?" I could tell he felt sorry for me, and it was at that moment I realized there was nothing to feel sorry about. Trust me, waiting tables is no less honorable than singing about hamburgers for a living. We have a hard time in America recognizing the honor of service, and it's not a winning part of our nation's personality.

THE "HIGH" FROM SERVING

A customer's praise and approval can be as intoxicating as the buzz one gets from the sound of an audience's applause. Believe me, I've been high on both.

Remember that **great service serves the server first**.

What I didn't yet have the perspective or hindsight to understand was that I had been given a choice and was fortunate enough to have made the right one. I began by doing what I encourage others to do now: Deal with what is right in front of you first.

Lee Cockrell, former executive vice president of operations for the entire Walt Disney World Resort always used the acronym WIN: "What's Important Now." As he writes in his book, *The Customer Rules*: "What's important now is not always immediately obvious." I agree, and I would add that the effect you have every time you deliver your best in service is not immediately obvious, either.

It is easy to "drown in circumstance" and feel overwhelmed by tasks. But instead of worrying about everything (e.g., getting another agent, having new photos taken, finding auditions, balancing the checkbook, panicking my family), I began to focus on bringing excellence to whatever was right in front of me.

Having the server job allowed me to aim at delighting one customer at a time, one moment at a time. I didn't have to figure out how to be the center square on the board of Hollywood Squares just then, I needed to be good at whatever task was in front of my face. One patron, one table, one transaction at a time. These moments, strung together, reset the context of my personal narrative—as they do for all of us, whether we're cognizant of the process or not.

After enough customers, patients, or clients respond to how nice you are, you'll find that you begin seeking out these opportunities the way children seek out sugar. When this motivation drives a work culture, one can also see amazing results. At that point, the customer's positive expectations can help sustain the performance of the servers.

People who like running know about the "runner's high," which is that feeling one gets after sustained physical exertion when our bodies provide a boost of endorphins. A similar high is available to those in service who continually strive to exceed expectations. There is a near instantaneous payback we feel from surpassing a client's expectations because it reinforces our **personal context**. We carry ourselves differently after each affirmation, making us more capable and confident of delivering additional wow-service moments. The power of this kind of self-investment is impossible to overstate.

Aligning yourself with this concept of exceeding expectation, until it is instinctual, is the key to providing outstanding customer experiences, and vital in inspiring others to do the same.

WOULD YOU BE INTERESTED IN WORKING AT DISNEYLAND?

We become how we act. Some of the people I've worked with over the years have been able to **think** themselves into a new way of acting, while some of us are better at **acting** our way into a new way of thinking. Either way, sooner or later, our experience meets up with our expectations. Behaving like a gracious server as often as possible had an eventual effect on me, and I steadily became a gracious server and enjoyed the advantage it provided.

Irrespective of the company we may work for, everything we do defines our personal brand. What we look like, sound like, smell like, and feel like to be around represents our brand no differently than a hotel lobby offers clues as to the guest experience one can expect. People often say you can't judge a book by its cover. Well, maybe so, but you can usually get a pretty good feel for what it's about.

Approaching every table with the objective of exceeding guest expectations did more than yield good tips. It also offered me continuous opportunities to redefine myself, one table, one customer, one check at a time. The work was exhausting but character-building for a hitherto spoiled brat.

Equally as honest and refreshingly unpretentious were the people I worked with. There was a kaleidoscope of personalities among my coworkers, many of whom were working their way through school or single parenthood.

I also found that non-showbiz people were significantly lower maintenance; infinitely easier to make laugh, entertain, get to know, and sincerely engage with than most of the show folk I'd been exposed to. The steakhouse restaurant, like Los Angeles itself, was quite the melting pot and definitely the most diverse environment I'd been a part of up to that point. We worked hard and played hard ... maybe harder.

After developing skills in both table waiting and leadership, I was ready to get serious, forget about performing (onstage anyway) and climb the corporate ladder at Stuart Anderson's company of Black Angus Steakhouses. It was a great company, and I was proud to be a part of the team and to become knowledgeable about the food and beverage business. I was happy marching around the restaurant like it was my own personal Disneyland to run.

My restaurant's location, I imagined, would set the benchmark for customer service and become The Happiest Black Angus on Earth. I was already confident that there was no business but show business, and since I'd been in show business most of my life already, this ambition should be easy to attain.

Then, after pretending to work at Disneyland for nearly five years, I got a phone call.

"Hey, Louie, I know this is out of nowhere, but would you be interested in working at Disneyland?"

(Great service serves the server first!)

CHAPTER TWO
FIRST TASK IN A MAGIC KINGDOM

WELCOME TO THE HAUNTED MANSION!

Full disclosure. My idea of "pretending" to work at Disneyland was, for me, hardly random. All things Disney spoke to my heart as a child—the movies, the cartoons, *Walt Disney's Wonderful World of Color* on television … but nothing grabbed my imagination quite like Disneyland. More on this later, but suffice it to say, on the day Walt Disney died (December 15, 1966), the principal of my elementary school came into my third-grade classroom to see if I was all right. Enough said, for now.

I am often asked if working at one of the Disney parks spoils the illusion and magic one feels as a paying guest. The answer is yes *and* no. No matter what aspect of traditional show business one examines, the contrast between on and offstage is almost always disarmingly stark. Most patrons of an elaborate Broadway musical would be shocked to know that the backstage of the theater they're sitting in (at $200 a seat) looks a lot like a recently condemned tenement built in the 1930s, featuring rickety fire escapes and quaint, four-letter-word graffiti inscribed by Julie Andrews or Nathan Lane. The same jarring experience awaits you the first time you catch a glimpse of Space Mountain with all the lights switched on, or witness Mary Poppins fighting with her boyfriend on a cellphone—it's disconcerting at first. However, one can also develop an even deeper appreciation for the operational and artistic labors involved with bringing the show to life on a daily basis.

My first gig at Disneyland was hardly a glamorous one, but it was a step back into performing again. My role required I be decked out in a whimsically elaborate, turn-of-the-century funeral director costume—replete with a black top hat, tailcoat adorned with a dead boutonnière—while speaking in a camp vampire accent. The assignment was to entertain the massive crowds that could often be stuck in line during the busy summer season as they waited to enter the Haunted Mansion attraction. This involved seven thirty-minute "comedy sets" per shift. There was a low brick wall in the center of the queuing area that became the stage where my character would improvise zany interactions with the guests. Consider this the bloody frontline of a battle called Show Business. It was like modern day vaudeville with no protection from the audience whatsoever. The shift was long, hot, and the guests could get surly.

I loved every minute of it.

This was not the first nor the last attempt Disney would employ to bring organically interactive characters into the themed "lands" of the parks. Rather than properties guests might recognize from their film library, Disney created characters that "lived" only within the realms of the Magic Kingdom. While this may sound like an easy fit for the park, it wasn't.

Throughout theme park history, a duality has existed.

There has always been a constant internal battle for balance and control between the worlds of **creation** and **operation**. By all accounts, this rivalry has existed since the first day of Disneyland's opening in 1955.

The folks in on the creative side want to try things that the professionals in operations find problematic. Operations wants and needs consistency. Creativity and consistency are not always conducive in the world of live entertainment, hence the subtle-yet-pervasive friction between the two factions lasting over half a century.

You can't blame the folks in operations. They're moving thousands of people within a confined space as efficiently and safely as possible. Wacky entertainers popping up out of nowhere and drawing stationary crowds requires a flexibility and spontaneity that park operations had not yet attained. Nor would they for quite some time—not before several more forays into the study of making this kind of entertainment work.

This was evidenced when, on my first day, I jumped onto my brick-wall stage only to be briskly hauled away by security personnel almost immediately, who demanded, "Who are you and what do you think you're doing?" The guards had not been informed by the creative folks that a wisecracking undertaker would be appearing that morning.

Undaunted, I went out for my second set with a strut. En route to the Haunted Mansion, I bowed to greet a little girl in a stroller. Her father mistook me in my top hat and tails for a different Disney character. "You know who that is, honey?" he said to the child. "Jiminy Cricket!" Nevertheless, I simply posed for a picture and pretended to be Jiminy Cricket so as not to embarrass the dad.

Disney service principles already in action!

Now, frustratingly, I wasn't technically a Disney cast member yet, only a contracted player hired through an outside agency that provided entertainment for the busy seasons. Barbara Epstein, who had directed and produced the longest running stage show in L.A.-theater history (A-*5*-*6*-*7*-*8*—*a Musical Revue*) and a former creative at Disney park productions was tasked with bringing interactive performance to Disneyland. A team of about twelve of us were dispatched throughout the park to various high-impact areas.

While still not really an official employee of Disney, it was good enough for me. This was a childhood dream come true. The entire troupe had to work hard, and the shifts were pre-union long. When not performing, I traversed the park studying, well, *everything*. All aspects of the enterprise fascinated me, and I wanted to learn as much as there was to know about how the park worked. Everything.

It was my good fortune to share a dressing room with the legendary African-American musical trio named the Royal Street Bachelors, who performed at an outdoor venue in New Orleans Square for over twenty years. Since the three jazzmen had shared the dressing room area for so many years, they had tricked the place out like a cross between the sets of *Home Improvement* and a James Bond movie. Cabinets rolled open to reveal musical instruments, healthcare and grooming products, TV controls, car tools, and extra sets of clothing. How they managed to get three full-sized "Lazy Boy" armchairs backstage I will never know. Helicopter, maybe?

At that time, the three musicians ranged in age between seventy-two and eighty, and they had been personally hired by Walt Disney himself. Each had performed at several of the park's venues and each had stories, anecdotes, and myths of Walt drawn from their own memories. They would regale me with stories of Walt dropping by the dressing room in the middle of the day just to talk, or how he would march around the park at all hours of the day or night to inspect it.

I did a lot of inspecting myself throughout that first summer working there in 1987, both onstage and off. However, the training I was to receive that would prove the most helpful in one day becoming a "customer service guru" didn't come from fellow cast members but from the guests themselves.

LISTENING TO THE TROOPS

The role customers and clients can play in creating and, especially, maintaining a service culture cannot be overstated. People will always find what they are looking for, and the expectations customers bring can shape your own service performance profoundly as well. Knowing your audiences' expectations is vital if you are to exceed them.

Since a bunch of us actors carpooled together from Hollywood to Anaheim for this gig each day and each started and finished our shifts at different times, it was not uncommon for us stay at the park for up to ten hours. This made for a long day, but it would allow a lot of time to wander around the resort and absorb.

One of my favorite things to do off the clock was to take the monorail over to the Disneyland Hotel bar and nurse a soft drink while listening to guests sharing their own family's adventures or, just as often, schemes and tactics for a successful day at the park.

There is an unquestionable difference between the typical Disneyland guest and the average Walt Disney World traveler. The audiences are quite different, and not in the way Walt expected. Disneyland's patrons consist of roughly 65 percent of folk living within a 200-mile radius, with the rest coming from out-of-state or international locales. The exact reverse is true of the Florida property. This is part of the reason the original California property has an audience base with a much stricter sense of ownership than its Floridian counterpart. A deeper reverence for the park exists as well, as many guests have strong ties from having made multiple childhood visits. Many know the place like the back of their hands and want existing things to stay the same forever! I sort of fall into this latter group. There is something accidentally perfect about Disneyland, which (to me) will always be the "real" one.

Walt Disney had anticipated that the Florida property would serve a more discriminating visitor who would be more likely to have seen more sophisticated, authentically historic destinations and might turn their noses up at faux realities. Not the case as it turns out. First, the average guest at the Florida property is so overwhelmed by its sheer size that it's easier for them to miss tiny flaws or inferiorities in the attractions. Secondly, on average, they will have visited much less often, and are not nearly as attached to the history and the way things are "supposed to be."

So, most of the patrons I was eavesdropping on during my off-time were seasoned Disneyland travelers who knew the drill. They all brought with them well-planned strategies and personal philosophies on "doing the park" successfully. As I would listen to these happy-yet-weary, travelers, their tales often took on the epic proportions of war stories. Most were of victory, but they occasionally conveyed struggle and defeat.

The interfamily dialogues I heard most often centered around three main topics:

How delighted they were with a specific show or attraction.

Park-going strategy.

The amazing guest service. Although average tourists did not use terms like "guest service" back then. They probably didn't use the term "waxing" either but you get my point. I could think of no other place of business where the customers sat around and tried to compete as to who had the best service story to tell. (Rather like fish-catching stories around a campfire or attendants of group therapy playing top-your-testimony.)

What the guests' stories seemed to have in common was how even their high expectations were consistently exceeded, usually involving what I was to come to know as "the personal touch" from one of the thousands of cast members. For most guests, it was the simple gestures and acts of kindness they felt so passionately about sharing with each other.

Even thirty years ago, the parks could get very crowded and difficult to navigate, especially with kids or guests with special needs. Cast members were taught to treat every guest as a VIP (very *individual* person) and seek out ways of making their visit happy, memorable, and if possible, easier. If there is one thing even the most ardent Disney fans will admit is that the parks occasionally require Herculean strength and patience, particularly for the uninitiated. Using the "troop" metaphor is not completely without merit, especially if you've ever been present at what they call the "rope drop" at the commencement of park hours (when the visitors flood in)—and it's not for the weak.

Remember what I said earlier about **context**?

Think about the dedication required of a vacationer who manages to get themselves and their entire family up and ready at the crack of dawn (or earlier) to be among the first allowed into the park on any given day. It's less a vacation, more a *mission* with a plan of attack, often years in the making, with a cost that can take even longer to save for. This is not a casual lark for the typical traveler. In fact, when they drop the rope, allowing throngs of guests to stampede to their first attraction, nobody's casually larking anywhere. No, they're competing! Competing with other families and overtaking those they consider weaker than their own. I'm not kidding: It's organized bedlam and an amazing thing to witness from the other side of the rope.

This special moment in the day is what Walt used to refer to as "The Opening Curtain," and your business or work-life has one too. The moment that customer expectations and your readiness collide creates the opening of *your* "show" and the beginning of *your* brand relationship; it's the moment when, on some level, customers agree to participate in the narrative of *your* business, *your* story. Your "opening curtain" may be opening the door to your own store or even simply making your grocery checkout lane available to customers at the start of your shift. Your show begins the moment any client or coworker can be affected by your presence.

Portraying Mortimer the Mortician outside the Haunted Mansion the summer of 1987 was to be my opening curtain for the show I'd share with Disney for most of the next two decades. The lessons I learned in that magical kingdom (from listening and watching both fellow cast members and guests) instilled in me and continue to provide **context**—the proscenium for the stage upon which my life's show plays out.

CHAPTER THREE
GO EAST, YOUNG MAN!

HOLLYWOOD EAST

It was not really our intention to move to Florida when we (my partner, John, and I) came to visit for the first time in the spring of 1989. However, as soon as we heard the voice (the same iconic voice heard all over Disneyland) saying, "Ladies and gentlemen, boys and girls, welcome to Orlando—*The City Beautiful*" piped through the speakers of the international airport, there was an eerie sense of destiny at play.

Fate availed herself once again in the guise of friend and Disney Entertainment Director Barbara Epstein. She had been hired to produce the musical sequences for the new Mickey Mouse Club being filmed at the soon-to-open Disney/MGM Studios theme park, and she brought John out to be her assistant for several weeks, allowing us to see the Florida resort for the first time. I was thrilled.

Looking back, moving to Orlando made perfect sense and should have been an obvious choice. *TIME* magazine had recently run a cover story heralding central Florida as the new "Hollywood East." Disney and Universal were both building working studios to lure production to the East Coast, and the parks were adding hundreds of (decent paying) performing jobs. Seemed like a pretty perfect fit. This may have been in the back of our minds during the vacation, but all we did initially was marvel at a place we had both wanted to see since we were children. (On my twelfth birthday, I obtained a paper route in order to buy Disney stock prior to the 1971 Florida resort's opening, so this was a long time coming.)

Like everyone, I was immediately overwhelmed by the sheer size of the property: forty-three square miles, or 2,700 acres, a high proportion of which was still untouched compared to the mere 200 acres of its West Coast counterpart. The entire Disneyland resort could fit in the parking lot of its sister Magic Kingdom, one of the four gargantuan parks contained within the resort.

We were able to attend a cast preview of the freshly minted Disney/MGM Studios park just days before it was unveiled to the public. Little did I know at the time how much time I was to spend in the place Disney CEO Michael Eisner referred to as "the Hollywood that never was and always will be." The trip had indeed been magical, and by the time the sun set behind the Cinderella Castle on our last evening, there was no question we were going to live and, hopefully, work there.

I had continued working at Disneyland during peak periods for two years, while simultaneously keeping the server job at Black Angus. Now the Disney gig was over, and I was over Los Angeles. To me, there was a palpable tension in Southern California; the vibe was turning nasty. One night, a patron with a machine gun came swooping into the restaurant and the staff had to huddle and hide in the employee restroom. That was enough, thank you, time to go. (Historic rioting engulfed the city hardly a year later.)

The amount of employment opportunity at Walt Disney World was nearly as stunning as the scale of the property. The area was growing exponentially and so was the need for skills of any and all kinds. Barbara was able to transfer John into the cast of a long running dinner show, but I had to wait *three months* for comedy-performer auditions.

That meant back to waiting tables for a while, this time on the tourist-frenzied International Drive at the now defunct Steak and Ale restaurant, which nearly required a chair and a whip just to get through a shift in one piece. The wage in Florida for tipped employees was $2.01 an hour at the time, so if you got stiffed by a large group of international businessmen on a $1,000 check (which happened frequently), it could literally cost me money to work after taxes were deducted. Those auditions couldn't come quick enough. Patience was in order, and I didn't have a lot on hand.

THE AUDITION

Finally, the day came when it was time to snag this dream. There was way too much at stake to blow this. John and I had already relocated, and for me failure was not an option. This area was not one of Ms. Epstein's domains, so I was going to have to win it without her help this time around.

Over 400 hopefuls of all ages, shapes, and sizes were in attendance the day auditions were held for comedic actors in Orlando. A seven-city tour was underway, and this was the last weary stop for a gaggle of show directors representing various stages across the resort. Most of them had endured hours of song and dance tryouts the prior day ... and it showed.

We had to wear large, numbered badges on our torsos. I was #100: the tenth person in the tenth group to be admitted into the audition room in one of the hotel convention centers. As I recall, the process took over three hours. (This was before the Actors' Equity Association came aboard the Disney juggernaut in 1991 and significantly streamlined this experience.)

Oddly, I possessed a curious serenity as I rose to deliver the monologue I had written for the audition. Most actors despise having to audition in a group, but I've always loved it, even as a child. Here's the thing: Being around other nervous people calms and focuses me. Not to sound like a jerk or a Marvel supervillain, but [*spoken in a deep, THANOS voice*]: "The smell of fear makes me stronger."

The sixty-second comedic piece involved a wild-eyed preacher bemoaning the horrors of cola addiction. Wearing my signature white short-sleeved shirt and dark bowtie, I stepped forward, and (as we say in showbiz) KILLED IT—like scoring straight tens in ice skating to win the gold. I remained calm and composed all the way to my car ... where I promptly cried like a three-year-old boy. A job was offered almost immediately, and a work relationship of nearly two decades began.

... Only it wasn't exactly the job I dreamed of or wanted.

A large number of new shows were opening that I fancied myself perfect for. Most were known as "scripted shows," requiring little to no improv (a skill I didn't feel was a strength yet), which seemed like a preferable option. However, being one of the few professional actors in America with experience in improvisational, interactive theater within a Disney theme park turned out to be a blessing and a curse.

I was cast in what was to be known for years as "Streetmosphere," performed on the faux Hollywood Blvd at Disney/MGM. This was slightly surreal, as I had actually lived on the real Hollywood Blvd in L.A., in close proximity to the authentic Chinese Theater, a duplication of which featured as the new park's hub. So weird.

The prospect of this gig frightened me for a number of very good reasons. Not only would it be hotter than Hades working outside in the Central Florida summers but also the word "experimental" was being bandied about way too often for my liking in reference to this new endeavor. This wasn't my first time at the rodeo, so I knew that in the theme park world, "experimental" typically translates to "temporary." No worries, it was a start.

A lot was different about working at the larger Florida enterprise, not the least of which was being a bona fide cast member this time, which meant experiencing the three-day orientation called Traditions. Other, more cynical participants would refer to this process as "pixie-dusting," which would have been just fine with me, but the experience went much deeper than that.

The backstage area, known as the Disney University (D.U.), looked like most of the behind-the-scenes locales designated for cast members. The architecture was quite reminiscent in look, smell, and feel of public school buildings designed in the late '60s or early '70s: clinical yet somehow "woodsy" inside and out. It really did feel like a plain, simple high school campus amidst what was still a vast, dense swath of Florida backwoods at the time.

Once entering, it took mere seconds for the average person to understand nobody was kidding around about any of this pixie dust stuff. Yet, I felt strangely at home, oblivious to the future relationship I was going to have with this building and its classrooms.

Historic and unique Disney artifacts were strategically littered around the halls and rooms: a scale model of a submarine, an animatronic pirate head, vintage Mickey Mouse dolls. It was a treasure trove for anyone with as much passion for Disney as I had.

There was something else at D.U. found everywhere: Walt. Pictures and recordings of the great man abounded within those walls, as well as many of his most cherished quotes. Everything in the building one could touch, hear, and see was designed to establish an emotional connection to the company and create a context for the launch of one's Disney career.

Usually, the first-day indoctrination into the Disney culture is spent within a flattened hierarchy. By that I mean everyone is on the same step of the ladder for the onboarding experience. Executives participate exactly as frontline food and beverage hosts on that first day. This is made abundantly clear at the outset. Anywhere from fifty to a hundred new-hires could be sitting around tables together, regardless of status. A new vice president could be sitting next to a new custodial worker, sitting next to a housekeeper who's sitting next to the new Peter Pan.

My experience was slightly different.

Since many of the singers, dancers, actors and variety artists from the audition tour were hired simultaneously, approximately sixty of them happened to be starting orientation on that same day, in that same room—just us. They formed a slightly surly group with a collective attitude not terribly different from a gang of clever seventh graders about to make life hell for a substitute teacher.

In all candor, the group consisted of an amazingly talented block of people who had come to Florida to be a part of Hollywood East. None of us were "green," or kids just out of school; mostly, we were seasoned performers with a few among us soon to star on television and Broadway, or already had. The ages ranged from twenty-five to seventy-two.

Suffice it to say, not all these fellow showbiz pros shared my unabashed, wide-eyed enthusiasm for hooking up with The Mouse. Many were used to a more, shall we say, bohemian and free-spirited workplace. More than a few brought a healthy dose of skepticism to what they considered to be a potential brainwashing session. It didn't take long for a conversion, almost all succumbing to the pixie-dusting.

The facilitator—a short, friendly but no-nonsense former character performer by the name of Anda—had certainly slayed greater dragons than us and was up to the challenge of taming and training a bunch of smart-aleck carnies.

My reputation, for better or worse, as a "Disnoid" among my entertainment peers was forever cemented on that day. Anda said, "I'm going to offer a special prize to the person who can answer a question nobody has ever got in one of my sessions." She paused, looked around the room with just the slightest trace of smugness and continued, "What was the name of Walt Disney's very first television series on—" ... before she could even finish the question, I blurted out, "DISNEYLAND. It was called Disneyland!"

Anda was so ill-prepared for this outcome that seemed to

have forgotten what the "special prize" was even supposed to be. No matter, for me, the prize was the instant respect and curiosity I suddenly received from my theatrical comrades. Some remained wary of me for a short time until they discovered my passion for Disney did not necessarily equate with being straight-laced … at all.

Many of the people who started with me that day (skeptical or not) became close friends. More than half enjoyed decades of steady employment there, and some are still with the company to this day, almost thirty years later—a few are still appearing in the same show!

A MAGIC KINGDOM IN A GOLDEN AGE

Employees fortunate enough to work for a company during one of the cyclical "golden ages" are rarely aware of it at the time. We were. The last decade of the twentieth century was an exciting time to be an employee of the Walt Disney Company. Bold expansion was the order of the day, and CEO Michael Eisner and (until his untimely passing) Frank Wells were leading the charge. The two seemed to have the Midas touch, since every corner of the company they worked with began printing money and beating all expectations.

It was all-hands-on-deck and a time chock-full of opportunity. New hotels, restaurants, parades, and attractions were springing up everywhere, and (maybe for the only time during my entire Disney tenure) money was no object at the company. Do it big or don't do it at all.

Disney had always enjoyed a reputation of promoting from within, so anyone with passion and skill could find plenty of avenues for growth. Many, many people share the experience of entering the organization in one area or department, then spending the bulk of their career in another discipline altogether.

For years, it seemed like the greatest launch pad for success at Disneyland was being a skipper on the Jungle Cruise attraction.

My role in the Streetmosphere troupe meant that I was essentially a "contract player" for the resort, the same way MGM studios had employed contract players in the '40s. This meant that on any given day, you could be assigned to one of myriad roles in multiple productions. The day worked similarly: You would arrive at the studio gate and a security guard would wave you in after confirming your name on a clipboard. Next, you reported to the wardrobe building, where a costume would be issued for the day's show. From that point on, the day is scheduled with precision and strictly organized to the minute. It was lot like working on a movie set, so you could say I found my "Hollywood East" after all.

STREETMOSPHERE

For most of the next twelve years I would be "anchored" at Streetmosphere.[1] Even during my entire training career with D.U. and the Disney Institute, I was to be employed within the entertainment department. At least one day a week would be spent performing in one of the multiple shows I was rehearsed in and approved for, no matter what was happening with training.

To put it bluntly, Streetmosphere was one of the weirdest

---

1 That title has since been trademarked by a casino conglomerate, right out from under Disney's nose. The Disney group is now called The Citizens of Hollywood.

jobs one could ever have at Disney, or anywhere. I was part of substantial a grab bag of versatile entertainers who could be dispatched anywhere at any time on the property. It was often madness. At one point, I could be bounced around over five shows AND do a parade or two during the span of a week.

However, my touchstone role at the resort for many years was portraying the movie mogul and mayor of our pretend Hollywood at Disney/MGM. Performers were heavily involved in the creation of our characters, and I named mine "Shelby Mayer" as a soundalike homage to the original MGM chief L.B. Mayer. The task was to weave in and out of scheduled shows while incorporating long-form interactive improvisation in between. As fun as we made it look, it could be very hard work, often in blistering heat. (One day I will write a separate book detailing my prolific and often bizarre experiences as a theme park performer. Just the stories of maneuvering drunken celebrities through staged interviews are enough for an entire chapter.)

The job was an equal measure of exhilaration and exhaustion. But there was a burning desire to do something else, and I couldn't stop thinking about my experience during the Traditions process and how it seemed to be summoning me.

CHAPTER FOUR
ATTENDING UNIVERSITY

THE PIXIE DUST FACTORY

As alluded to earlier, the training and development hub known as Disney University (D.U.) was considered (by some) to be the "Pixie-Dust Factory." A few dismissed it as a place where new employees became glossy-eyed converts with a more-than-rosy outlook about what awaited them in the real world of selling happiness, and to be fair, this was true for some. Knowing what I know now, it would have been wise to better prepare new-hires for the potential stress of selling fun. There was indeed both salesmanship and showmanship involved in the training and induction of new cast members as they joined the Disney "family," which does sound a lot like a conversion, I admit.

The Traditions program was and is, above all else, an **invitation to believe** in the culture with a binary choice to participate or not. Additionally, no one left orientation without understanding the values of the organization, its priorities, or what was expected of them. The "why" was made implicitly clear, which was the foundational goal anyway. The objective remains engaging new employees to feel they are now part of the Disney "story." In fact, the very first activity of the training day identifies participants as Disney characters representing the brand exactly as Mickey does.

The trainers (or "Traditions Assistants" as they were known for a reason no one could figure out) consisted of primarily frontline cast members, representing the many areas and departments of the resort. They were borrowed from every location for the span of one year to serve as part of a diverse group of about twenty-five trainers. They joined a group of permanent full-time HR individuals tasked with training and development of the nearly (at the time) 60,000 cast members—the largest single-site employer in America. As of 2019, that number tipped 80,000.

With my passion for all things Disney and my performing background, a trainer role should have been an obvious fit, right? Well, maybe not.

UM, NO …

Each fall, Disney would start the ardent selection process for their squad of Traditions Assistants. Over 300 people would apply annually (out of 35,000 cast members in 1990 and 65,000 as of 2017), and each one was interviewed before starting a long selection process of several stages. This exercise was for hardcore Disney folk, expected to represent the brand in much the same way the resort's Disney Ambassadors conducted themselves when traveling for press junkets with Mickey and the gang. One was expected to represent the Disney "look" at all times and know Disney history going in—clearly a prerequisite.

It took the second year of my employment for me to feel ready to throw my hat in.

As confident as I felt going into my appointed interview, upon arrival I had an immediate sense of not quite being in sync. Of the seven or so gentlemen sitting in the waiting area, I was the only applicant not wearing a navy-blue suit—the single "stylishly gray" suit in the bunch. It was almost like that scene in *A Wrinkle in Time* in which all the kids in one neighborhood look and move alike. What was I thinking? Had I forgotten about appropriate *costuming* for an audition?

When it was finally my turn to meet the Poppins-like, practically-perfect-in-every-way interviewer, I enthusiastically took my chair and readied myself for whatever probing question I was about to be thrown. How big was the resort? What was the first Mickey Mouse cartoon? Who did his voice? What are the four "pillars of excellence" in the organization? Bring it—I was ready.

The first (and only) question posed was, "Why do you think Disney is so successful at creating magical moments for our guests?" *Really? That's the question? Why are we so good?* This seemed rather a banal question for the proceedings but okay.

My honest and, I thought at the time, artful answer was, "Well, at this point I think our guests are doing a lot of this work for us. Because of the efforts of cast members over a period of many years, our guests already **believe in us** when they get here. Most of them approach us, anticipating a friendly 'Disney encounter,' which makes it easier to deliver one."

The instant, unguarded reaction to my answer from the no-hair-out-of-place young woman was a perplexed look. "Well, isn't that an interesting way to look at things. It was so great to meet you, Louis," said the woman with a disarmingly serene smile. I'd been to enough auditions in my life to know what that meant: "Thanks, but no thanks." This would also not be the last time I would receive disappointing news delivered with a Stepford-Wives smile of tranquility while working at Disney.

IF AT FIRST YOU DON'T SUCCEED ...

The following year was different. First, I charged a navy-blue suit I couldn't really afford to my Dillard's credit card (a suit that lasted several years and about two hundred presentations!). Secondly, rather than the private, austere interview, the three hundred-plus applicants had five minutes to tell a story about their most important "Disney moment," one at a time in groups of twenty. The program had been taken over by a fellow Californian and unabashed Disney fan by the name of Steve Riley. Steve had started at Disneyland in merchandise while still in high school, and hard work and focus had made him an important player in training and development.

Overwhelmingly, the hopefuls had no prior stage experience, nor had many of them ever spoken in front of people. But diverse in every way, the crowd was a true cross section of the property.

Remember what I wrote earlier about the super-strength that comes over me whenever I smell fear? Well, when it was my turn to get up and speak, I told a story about the first time I ever stood on a stage, which was also the first day I'd ever laid eyes on Disneyland. Towards the end of my story, with no theatrics intended, I began to get choked up and had to hold it together. It was a genuine moment and was perceived as such by the panel of interviewers. They were looking for applicants with passion, credibility and, yes, showmanship—stars had aligned. So began the most profound and exhilarating period in my Disney career.

I continued to share that story again and again, literally hundreds of times as a Disney facilitator and professional speaker. No matter the program, client, industry or event, I continue to this day to close the presentation with this life-changing memory. It is not uncommon for me to still get choked up at the end.

LANDING IN A LAND OF HARDCORES

"Do *you* know the name of Goofy's nephew?" queried one of the new members of the Traditions team to another as I signed in the first morning of what was to be six weeks of intense preparation to be the day-one trainer of new cast members. I was among serious "Disnoids"—no question about it, this was truly the land of the hardcore fans.[2]

Like the applicants, the new team represented a wide cross section of employees. Among others, we had a custodian, a finance manager, monorail driver, costumer, food and beverage hostess, window decorator, gardener, and a Prince Charming who could/would demonstrate the official parade wave at the drop of a hat.

Between the ages of twenty-two and seventy, we all had a strong connection to the place and the brand, and most of us probably already considered ourselves "brand ambassadors" going in. Despite representing every size, age, and ethnicity, we all still looked as though we could have toured with the *Donnie & Marie* show or (for those of you who remember)

---

2 For the record, Goofy's nephew is named Gilbert.

the group Up With People. The term "clean-cut" might be an understatement—at least on the outside.

There was the usual, unspoken ritual of sizing each other up, just like any other first day of school or employment. However, it wasn't long before the collective consciousness was one of support rather than competitiveness and many people in that room went on to be life-long friends and, in some cases, business associates.

We were challenged with learning an eight-hour presentation and becoming experts in detailing Disney history, language, and values, so I was a little surprised to discover that, besides myself, almost none of the new recruits possessed any experience in public speaking whatsoever. This was not by accident. Authenticity was considered the most valuable asset, and speaking skills could be taught. In fact, I was the only new member to come from the entertainment department. There were concerns that professional entertainers could easily slip into slickness when sincerity was preferred. Sincerity has always been one of the program's priorities since its inception in the mid-1950s.

A BRIEF HISTORY OF
THE UNIVERSITY OF DISNEYLAND

Should you find yourself at Disneyland one day, look up at the windows along Main Street USA. You'll eventually glimpse a notice that reads:

VAN ARSDALE FRANCE
Founder and Professor Emeritus
Disney Universities

It is a rare honor to "get a window" on Main Street, and it is reserved for only the most influential Disney Legends. Such is the case with a gentleman known as Van France, the undisputed father of Disney training. He wrote a book entitled *Window on Main Street* (now out of print) that chronicles the birth of what became known as the University of Disneyland.

People are often surprised to learn that many of Disneyland's "founding fathers" entered the scene by way of the military or companies contracted by the military. From ship-building to aerospace training, these men brought skills essential to building structures and cultures very quickly. C.V. Wood, Admiral Joe Fowler, France, and others stayed with Disney for many years and were known as the pioneers of theme park creation.

Mr. France's book, along with hours of archived interviews, reveals a scrappy rough-around-the-edges fellow who would not have come out of Central Casting as someone responsible for "Disney Magic." Rarely without a cigarette in hand, Van shared with most of the other founders a dry wit and extremely "wet" lunches. In the book, he makes clear he always kept a bottle of Scotch in a desk drawer "in case of emergencies." My guess is there were a whole lot of emergencies those first few years.

France had recently left Texas where he'd worked for an aircraft manufacturer, in charge of training. "I had created programs for Rosie the Riveter and other people in heavy industry, but here I was developing a program for people operating a crazy dream," he says in his book. He knew how to create quickly and specifically, which was excellent because no flowchart existed that combined so many different business units working in tandem—like the military.

France may have been one of the first people to use the term "soft-touch over high-tech" in reference to training. His presentations were oddly lacking in "flash," instead focusing on heart. "Mostly flip charts and felt boards were what we used." This is the era in which France is credited with creating "Disney Speak." No matter the task, "cast members" were "onstage" or "offstage" and would be known as "hosts or hostesses." They didn't have customers, they had "guests," and "costumes" were worn, not uniforms.

The original training site for Disneyland was less than auspicious—hardly a "university." Campus consisted of a small cluster of old homes at the undeveloped end of the property (later to become the Disneyland Hotel). In some cases, the houses were there because the owners refused to sell; others were sold with a lease allowing the owners to stay until they either moved or died.[3]

The two-story home originally owned by the Vandenburg family was freshened up and painted, becoming the so-called "The White House," so that it was easier for new-hires to find. Training took place there from 1955 until 1962 when it was moved to … a trailer.

Frankly, it wasn't until the unexpected death of Walt in 1965 that the training programs became truly institutionalized and consistent across all disciplines. The object changed from being a part of what Walt Disney was *dreaming* to what Walt *dreamed*;

---

3 One large patch of land that Disney desperately wanted was a strawberry field very near the park, but the owner was a stubborn patriarch with no interest in selling at all. For over fifty years the company made unsuccessful offers for the field. "I just don't want to," the owner would say. "Look, I know my kids are gonna sell it the minute I die, but I don't need to and I don't want to." He was right about the kids—they sold, and part of Disney's California Adventure exists on the site today.

hence, training for new cast members from that moment on became known as Traditions.

It was believed that training and development needed to be an ongoing way of life and a full-time university was required. This was named the University at Disneyland. In 1967, a young consultant named Mike Vance took the reins in California, while Van France went to Florida to prepare for the opening of Walt Disney World. It would be fair to say that Mr. France **normalized** the way Disney employees were trained, while Mr. Vance **formalized** it. The basic structure of the Traditions program remains strikingly similar to the post-Disney version instated in the late '60s.

CROSS-UTILIZATION

Part of the genius of the preparation process for Traditions teachers was the training designed to give each facilitator a working knowledge of areas across property. In the span of a few weeks, one could get on-the-job orientation with housekeeping, custodial, laundry, front gate, food and beverage, retail, and even the costume department (bringing characters "to life" for a set). The program gave every one of us a better appreciation of the tasks performed by the cast, and it wasn't easy work.

Have you done the laundry from fifteen resort hotels in a day? How about cleaning a hotel room completely trashed by a single pizza? Ever considered what it would be like to follow a horse with a broom and pan during the three o'clock parade? Trust me, there's a side to Disney World few people want to see.

While trainees did not get enough time to garner any real expertise in any of the assorted "roles," the cross-utilization (C.U.) training did offer an overview and perspective almost no one else got to experience. C.U. training also enabled future trainers to get to know their audience up close and personal, if only for a short while.

The "learning opportunity" I enjoyed the least (cleaning hotel bathrooms) was not the task I least excelled in. That distinction goes to the fifteen minutes I spent trying to sew the names of guests onto the back of Mickey Mouse ears. I say fifteen minutes because that's exactly how long it took to recognize I possessed virtually no aptitude for the assignment whatsoever and was pulled after destroying three pairs.

What I gleaned most from C.U. training was learning to identify the trait that differentiated great employees from average ones—INTENTION. This is where I became convinced that, in training, **context** would always be more important than **content**. Articulating the power of intention is the first skill we'll tackle together as we hone the ten skills of the service superhero.

LEARNING MY LINES

An eight-hour day is a long time to hold someone's attention, and it's also a lot of content to learn in a short period. A framework was employed—that I continue to use in my own business—in which the program is written out in full script form, but only used as a guide. Trainers are instructed to not even attempt to memorize the lines as written, but rather to learn the story arc of the day and the flow of important parts. This is a hard concept to grasp for some people who may not be comfortable with taking information and "making it their own" to deliver.

This was the pre-PowerPoint age. It is almost impossible to imagine now, but not a single slide was projected throughout the entire class, and very little video material was shown. Most of the first day centered around a dozen "show cards," illustrated with various characters, made of laminated cardboard and displayed on an easel—totally "soft touch." Important information was encouraged to be conveyed anecdotally whenever possible; essentially, the most important skill was storytelling. The training programs I have designed rely heavily on these methods as well. When casting a team of facilitators, the natural ability to tell an interesting story is most important—content can be taught. This was the philosophy of the Traditions program from its inception.

Beyond this straightforward delivery, only three short videos were shown in class. The day ended with a video entitled *Making Magic—It's What We Do*, that made me cry in the back of the room practically every time, just as I was to close out the day.

Since many in the "Trad Team" would represent the company and the university at various functions, we received much of the same training as the resort's Disney Ambassadors. Much of this training had to do with our behavior outside of the D.U. building, especially the way we *looked*.

One of the most memorable and useful days of the preparation process was the session conducted by the Disney-look specialist, an impeccably groomed woman with a cheery but no-nonsense style. Frankly, every kid in high school ought to take a course like this. It covered how to dress professionally on a budget, how to detect clothing that would not be durable, and memorable tidbits, such as, "Always dress one step and only one step above your audience" and, my favorite, "A sport coat can be worn with anything—but a **suit is a suit until it dies!**"

As we readied for our first day of facilitating, we also spent time with animators, imagineers and marketing executives. It is not an exaggeration to suggest we were some of the most informed employees on the property regarding the company and what was going on at any given moment.

TEACHER'S FIRST DAY

When I was selected to be first of our team to "open" with an actual class, I spent the week prior being incredibly nervous. Yet, on my first day as a Traditions instructor, I found it was one of the most naturally easy things I'd ever done. As if I'd done it hundreds of times before, there was an undeniable sense of belonging.

What was more challenging were the duties that took place before class, after class, and during break time. Trainers were responsible for up to one hundred people at a time … and their individual needs. At this time, the men were required to wear jackets and ties and be devoid of any facial hair or visible tattoos. Women could not wear eye shadow, and skirts could be no shorter than one inch above the knee and earrings no bigger than a nickel. No tattoos for the ladies either. Since we would be onstage and visible to guests at some point, our day would start with a welcome that covertly checked for compliance problems. There was never a welcome that did not find any "offenders."

We had a very large cloakroom that housed long racks of blue sport coats and generic gray slacks in every size we could borrow for the day. This harried portion of the day felt exactly like what is was: getting dozens of "kids" ready for school in thirty minutes.

Let's not forget … HAIR. Disney was very strict on this issue and had photos on display representing "good show/bad show." This was the sticky part, especially with young men who thought they'd test the boundaries. Sorry, non-negotiable! And don't even try the but-Walt-had-a-moustache routine because it wasn't going to work. You were simply sent home and rescheduled. (However, I know I wasn't the only facilitator who dug into their pocket to send a kid who obviously couldn't afford a haircut discreetly to the "Kingdom Cutters" and turned a blind eye to their tardy start time.)

Walking the trainees briskly down Main Street for a discussion at the castle was often a nightmare too because, like kids, you'd have "roamers," and losing somebody was not an option.

Over the next few years, I would come to recognize common archetypes among the participating new hires. There were the enthusiastic, the suspicious, the earnest, the cynical. There were people in class who were obviously "lifers" (you could see it in their eyes), while others weren't going to make it past the second time someone asked them where the bathrooms were. Regardless, there were two things that never ceased to amaze me.

No one forgets their first-day Traditions facilitator—ever. For over a decade after I no longer taught the class, people would still introduce themselves and remind me of a Traditions story they never forgot.

For some weird reason I could never figure out, many of us were routinely hit on during breaks or, more often, at the end of day. Is it a *teacher thing*? (I kind of get that, since my first crush was a teacher.) I was flattered but already in a relationship, so I would just go red-faced and goofy.

IT'S EVIL, MAN!

We weren't really supposed to take the throng of new hires on an attraction that first day in the park, but sometimes I just couldn't help but deviate from the approved walking-tour route. Actually, I became rather famous for deviating from many parts of the curriculum. I always "got away with it," with the exception of one tiny mishap.

One particular tour, the Magic Kingdom was unusually quiet, and I got the bright idea to slip my group into the queue for the Haunted Mansion since there was no line at that moment. *Perfect*, I thought, calculating that I could get the entire class through the attraction in about seventeen minutes. "Follow me!" I announced and shuffled off like Willy Wonka through the chocolate factory. My magical detour seemed to be working swimmingly until I detected a small commotion coming from the back of the queue. A panicked young man in his late teens ran up to me yelling, "There's a lady back there totally FREAKING OUT. She says the devil's in here, and she won't move!" A middle-aged Haitian woman, recently hired for housekeeping, was wild-eyed and on her knees, clutching one of queue posts while exclaiming, "This is evil, man! EEEVIL, man! I no go! I no goooo!" So much for flying under the radar. I leapt as quickly as I could to comfort her and guarantee I'd guide her out safely. There was just one problem; the only way out was forward, which meant I had to take the lady's hand and gently lead her onto the moving ride vehicle ("Doom-Buggy" as it's called) console her and beg her to trust me as we endured the dark-ride attraction together. It felt like the longest six minutes of my life, as this poor woman was convinced she was seeing dead people swirl out of graves while playing musical instruments.

"Maybe you should shut your eyes," I suggested, which would have been impossible since her eyes were now the size of Ping-Pong balls. Lamely, I tried to offer, "See? It's really rather pretty." This did not help and, instead, seemed to prove that I was, Beelzebub's kin. "Pretty?" she asked in horror. "PRETTY?!"

I was completely ignorant of the Haitian culture's long ingrained fear of voodoo in some circles. As far as this poor woman was concerned, I was truly dragging her on a motorized trip through Hell and neither of us could wait until the ride was over. Finally, after what seemed an eternity, the buggy came to a stop and I hustled her and the rest of the group offstage as quickly as possible. "Well, I think we all learned something about the diversity of our audience today," I said in a laughable attempt at recovery—we moved on.

The next morning, as I was walking though one of the university corridors, my coach Steve addressed me: "I hear we made a special side trip on the tour yesterday." The look of shame and sheepishness on my face seemed to be apology enough, so I was let off the hook and *never* took the "haunted detour" again.

YOU CAN STAY

After almost one hundred Traditions classes, my year on the Trad Team was coming to an end. The term was traditionally one-year only because it was a burden on the areas of the park we were borrowed from, and it ensured freshness in the program, But things were different for me and a lady by the name of Sheila Smith-Ward, as we were made coaches and trainers of the next two Trad Teams.

We participated in the auditions, selection process, and teaching the content of the program. I usually covered the story of Walt's life and legacy. For the rest of the year, Sheila and I would act as coaches and, occasionally, do some team facilitation with the fresh group. Helping people develop their presentation skills remains one of my very favorite things to do.

Staying on for an additional two years allowed us two other major opportunities. The first was serving on the team tasked with refreshing and reorganizing the first-day training program. Perhaps no other Disney work experience proved to be more valuable in the long run than taking the Traditions program apart and putting it back together again, benefitted by some first-rate mentoring.

The second opportunity, also especially significant and exciting for me, was to be part of something brand new that they were going to call the Disney Institute.

CHAPTER FIVE
FROM INSTITUTE TO INSTITUTION

THE BIG IDEA

If one were to use only a single word to describe the era in which Michael Eisner was the CEO of Disney it would have to be "big." Or, more precisely, "BIGGER"! Eisner didn't like doing anything small: big movies, big parks, big structures, and big, bold ideas. Birthing his ideas was usually a greater challenge than he originally envisioned, and the Disney Institute is a fine example of a difficult labor.

The story goes that Mr. and Mrs. Eisner were big fans of a learning center/camp called the Chautauqua Institution, located on a beautiful lake in the woods located in southwest New York state. This was an upscale retreat for vacationing families spending "intellectual getaways" together. Families could study art, literature, rock climbing, religion, and cooking, among other things, while enjoying a remote, natural setting. Why not bring something like this to Disney? There had to be the perfect nook within the vast environs of the Florida property, right?

In theory, this seemed like a marvelous idea. However, as was occasionally the case, Michael's very privileged upbringing made it difficult for him to realistically anticipate the desires of his everyday audience. In his 1999 memoir, *Work in Progress*, Eisner admits to growing up with a slightly skewed sense of the world, assuming everyone dressed formally for dinner and had both an apartment in the city and a vacation home. This may have been why it was difficult to convince him that the demographic most likely attracted to a learning destination like Chautauqua would probably be the audience most likely repelled by the idea of a week among theme parks. Equally important was the fact that nobody was coming to Disney as a family with the intent of studying Cantonese cuisine either. What we knew about our audience should have shaped our curriculum, but it did not. The leadership team took to recreating Chautauqua more literally.

The pristine and well-manicured campus was nestled among what had been known as the Tree House Villas, where new executives were often housed during their relocation process. Beyond being beautiful, it had well equipped classrooms, kitchens, indoor and outdoor performance spaces, plus a restaurant and small movie theater. Everything was mint condition, and money appeared to be no object.

Disney was already making good money delivering customized corporate offerings out of the Disney University. I know this because I had already been a part of these programs and delivered dozens of presentations to high-end corporate clients about Disney's training practices and philosophies. Therefore, many of us involved assumed we would be a perfect fit for the new Disney-learning offerings. We were quite wrong.

The truth is that the launch team of the Disney Institute

didn't seem to want to have anything to do with us whatsoever. In fact, at first, they didn't seem to want to have anything to do with *Disney* at all, except the name and reputation. The price of a Disney Institute vacation did not even include admission into the parks! So, what was the point of it being on resort property? This would prove to be a serious miscalculation about potential visitors. We could have told them—we tried to tell them. Some of us who already had experience tried explaining to the development team that their audience would most likely consist of hardcore fans of the brand. I believed that the very name "Disney Institute" implied that they would actually be learning *about* Disney during the experience. Therefore, instead of ignoring where we were, we should have been *exploring* where we were. That is exactly what the guests wanted but were not offered.[4] "There should be a course all about the creation of our audio-animatronics," I remember imploring, "where they can actually program one of the figures to move and talk!" Theme park design, Walt's life, the transportation system, the "underground city" beneath the Magic Kingdom, putting fireworks shows together—all were suggested topics and potential courses and all were rebuffed. To be honest, my ego was a little bruised at how our input was dismissed.

Sometimes there is no joy in being right about something. With or without joy, many of us had, indeed, been correct about the guests' reaction to the Disney Institute during its first incarnation. We had also accurately predicted the universal annoyance of visitors being expected to buy park admission after

---

4 There were other examples of this mindset popping up all over the place. Disney's Animal Kingdom was initially another instance of giving guests what we thought they *should* want rather than what they *did* want.

purchasing a very pricey all-inclusive holiday. And, as suspected, they didn't really want to know that much about Cantonese cooking after all. The only truly popular course was about (you guessed it) Disney. Participants could learn about the history and mechanics of Disney animation with instruction on how to draw Mickey. Quickly the institute began to do something almost unthinkable on Disney property—lose money.

Not long afterward, reason and sanity prevailed and the professional business development programs from D.U., like DAQS (**D**isney's **A**pproach to **Q**uality **S**ervice), became the heart and soul of the Disney Institute. Today, its only focus is professional development in one form or another, and companies from all over the world continue to invest considerable time and money for Disney's insights. Cooking classes are no longer offered.

YOU'RE BEING A SILLY LITTLE MAN

There was no logical reason I should have found myself doing what I was doing. I had a high school education (graduating with not particularly auspicious grades), no college education to speak of (one class in stage makeup), no training in human resources or educational design. And yet I found myself helping to create and deliver world-class programs in customer service at the Disney Institute, offering guidance to some of the greatest brands in the world.

These amazing opportunities came to me primarily due to the same three things that will bring opportunity to you: **Intention**, **Service**, and **Gratitude**. It is when these three elements are in play that our dreams find us.

My friend Sheila and I continued to train the trainers, work on new products for the institute, deliver presentations to corporate clients, AND maintain our roles in entertainment (I was portraying movie mogul Shelby Mayer at the studio park, while Sheila kept her night gig at Disney's Pleasure Island).

The segments of the corporate programs she and I did were modular by design and could act as stand-alone presentations as well. This was among the reasons clients began requesting we be loaned out to deliver presentations at their headquarters and conventions. Disney was not particularly interested in "renting out" their facilitators, preferring instead to book packages at the resort, which brought in a lot more revenue. Eventually Toys"R"Us made them an offer they couldn't refuse, so Ms. Ward and myself found ourselves traveling for the company and delivering what I continue to call "speaking concerts."

This enterprise must have been profitable because, before long, the company had no qualms whatsoever about renting out their facilitators elsewhere. Many former institute "professors" used this experience to start their own independent businesses—myself included. I was so grateful and proud to have this opportunity that I never stopped to consider how much revenue we were bringing in as paid speakers. That is, until a certain client thought they would take me out to dinner and enlighten me.

BMW of Canada had been a recent client at the Disney Institute and requested my help in a presentation designed to prepare and enthuse their sales team for an upcoming car show. Car shows were in a transitional period from being an excuse for indulging salesmen to being more practical—they actually wanted to sell more cars at these events. I was thrilled to create a short program to deliver on a three-city tour through eastern

Ontario. This was in January, and I was astonished to learn how cold planet Earth could get.

After the last meeting, the regional director of sales and marketing took me out to dinner to celebrate and "discuss something." Approximately five seconds after the drink order was taken, my host launched into his well-thought-out presentation.

"Look, this isn't really any of my business," he started. "However, I just found out what your pay arrangement is for these talks and, well, I think you're being taken advantage of." I was shocked and speechless as he continued, "I won't tell you how much we paid to have you come and present, but I will tell you that if you don't look into going out on your own, then you're a silly little man."

No client had ever brought up my compensation before, and I had no idea how to respond to his remarks or take his advice. While he was correct that there was no extra compensation for these services, his assessment that I was getting the short straw was not one I shared. However, the older I become, the more I realize that lots of things can be true at the same time. I was receiving about 5 percent of the fees charged for trekking through the Canadian cold to speak that winter of 2001, but it was also true that the job provided me an education that money could never have bought. Let's be clear: I barely attended class in high school and went to college for about twelve hours in total. Still, the wisdom attained from hard work in the restaurant business continued to remind me of my axiom: **an investment of yourself is an investment in yourself**. The more I invested of myself, the more Disney invested in me, creating value I would take with me forever. Service had led me to this opportunity; service would guide me to the next one.

Most of you drawn to this book and its message will be, on some level, already in tune with the power of self-investment. I know that focusing on the positive attributes of service can be extremely difficult if you find yourself underpaid or undervalued by your employer—which is probably most of us. When we feel taken advantage of, the temptation to fall into resentment can be nearly overwhelming. This is poison. In these situations, one of the greatest skills of the service superhero is the ability see things through the eyes of the customer.

Think of the customer's eyes like the lens of a camera, capturing their experiences like scenes in a movie. Doing this can help most of us realign with our jobs rather than our tasks only.

Don't ever allow yourself to feel taken advantage of. Remember that you can take everything you **know** with you.

TIME FOR MY CURTAIN CALL

As the facilitators at Disney Institute were exposed to more and more visiting corporate clients, invitations to leave Disney for recruitment elsewhere became more and more frequent for many of us. My stock reaction was consistently, "I'm still really proud and happy to be a part of the Disney family," and I meant it without a single trace of irony or dishonesty.

Nevertheless, one specific encounter stuck out, which would prove to be pivotal and life-changing down the road. Not long after the "Canadian tour," a man and woman from Bank of America caught up with me after a program and said, "If you ever decide to go out on your own and do consulting, we'd love to be your first client. Sure wish you were free now—we're trying to mount a whole new initiative on customer service." I took their card and put it in my wallet without too much afterthought.

John and I were about to take off on what had almost become an annual trip to Hawaii. We made five trips, focusing on a different island each time and always ending with the same ritual. On the last sunset of the vacation, one of us would take the video camera and ask the other, "Is it time to go home now?" at which point the answer was always, "Yup, time to get back home." End of video, end of holiday. But at the beginning of 2001, as the sun was setting on our final day of a getaway to Kauai, John asked, "Well, are you ready to go home now?" Looking into the camera I responded thoughtfully, "You know … *not really.*" As it turned out, neither was he.

CHAPTER SIX:
LEAVING A GILDED CAGE (AND LEARNING TO FLY)

YOU'LL BE HERE FOREVER!

If it isn't already obvious, my respect, fondness, and gratitude for the Walt Disney Company is foundational to who I am as a person. However, the strong culture and the sense of security it provides can, in fact, ultimately morph into a gilded cage. It's beautiful and cozy on the inside, but there is a subtle confinement that can make the idea of trying to fly away unimaginable for some.

Actors and performers especially tended to cocoon themselves within the security and structure Disney provided. Where else could an entertainer find a job in which, in a lot of cases, they never had to audition again? The lure of complacency is strong. Over time it becomes increasingly difficult to contemplate leaving.

Even after leaving, the company's culture has a way of pulling you back "home." After my first twelve years with Disney, I left for seven years but came back again for another seven, finally leaving permanently in 2014.

The reason I left Walt Disney World the first time (after twelve years) had nothing to do with the Disney Institute whatsoever. My experiences with training and development continued to be challenging and satisfying, yet this was not where my true ambition ever really lay.

The entertainment department remained my home base; it was where I felt most valuable. It was also where my "dream job" within the company resided—show director. More specifically I wanted to get involved with coordinating and directing the "spectacles" on property: pyrotechnic shows, parades, water pageants and such. This would be quite a reach, I knew, for someone with my lack of formal education, so I found small projects and events around the property to take charge of and direct, hoping to prove myself and gain favor.

I was already a "lead" at our stage and frequently made responsible for tiny events like the unveiling of a name change for a restaurant, internal message videos, cast update presentations, or anniversary celebrations. This was a manner in which many future show directors got a start on the ladder then.[5]

An opportunity became available which seemed a perfect fit—directing a small cast of "warm-up" solo entertainers who performed before the Indiana Jones stunt show. Having done this kind of work before, I confidently tossed my figurative hat into the ring. Frankly, I felt good about my chances.

Returning from the Hawaii trip (the one where we weren't sure we wanted to come home), I immediately detected a squirrelly vibe from my fellow castmates and noticed no one was making direct eye contact. Had something awful happened

---

5 This is definitely not the protocol now for Disney theme park entertainment directors. Today, the company asks you for a masters degree to even be considered, or they contract directors from the outside.

while I was gone that nobody wanted to tell me about? Finally, after a couple of hours, my friend and castmate Annie (known for her candor) pulled me aside.

"Okay, I'm just gonna tell you," she blurted, "you didn't get the directing gig—they gave it to Herbie." Herbie was a fellow performer with a strong directing background, the choice was not weird at all. Still, I'd made a steady effort for almost twelve years and was frustrated enough to ask a young supervisor by the name of Matt why I'd been passed over again and how I could better my chances in the future.

He tried consoling me. "Now, you've got remember," began my leader, who looked like he'd just escaped from a boyband, "Herbie's been here a lot longer than you and, let's face it, you're not going anywhere. You'll be here forever!" He really should have stopped after the first point. While it was a fact that Herbie had put in more time (he's a very talented person, by the way, and friend to this day) Matt's second assumption would prove to be incorrect.

There was something about the cavalier line reading of "You'll be here forever" that separated my Disney experience into before and after. Suddenly, I recognized I'd become someone casually referred to as a "lifer." For the first time, I felt taken for granted and the words of the Canadian BMW exec of "silly little man" went from the back of my mind to the front.

Upon hearing the news Annie was good enough to provide me with, I actually felt *relief.* A bright smile came over my face that bewildered my confidant. "What?" she asked. My response was: "We're moving to Hawaii!" Promptly, I picked up the phone and made the same pronouncement to John who, frankly, didn't seem that surprised.

ALOHA!

"Moving to Hawaii seems like a really practical idea," said no one ever. And yet, these words sprang from my lips repeatedly to astonished friends and family over the spring of 2001 as we readied to pack everything we owned onto a steamship. On paper it did seem like a pretty good idea, actually, and not nearly as capricious an adventure as it sounded.

Since I was striking out on my own as a public speaker and service consultant, why not Hawaii? The state has a massive business convention industry and is filled with service employees from hotels, restaurants, and attractions. I believed I would be the only resident on Maui with the Disney credentials and experience, removing the price of flying someone in from the mainland. Much of the cost of booking a speaker involves travel, and there would be no travel expenses! Hawaii could be my niche, I thought. Pretty darn smart, right?

Also, we were fortunate enough to be financially ready for this kind of risk since, from the beginning, a large percentage of our salaries were being deducted and invested in the employee stock purchase plan. We had no children, and our house was nearly paid for, which allowed me to calculate that, once there, we could go nine months to a year without a job before we had to worry about money. Our move to Orlando had been easy and marked with good fortune, why wouldn't it be the same in Ka'anapali?

As it turned out, it wasn't the same experience at all. We weren't naïve in the sense that we already knew living in a tourist destination was vastly different from visiting one: There is a unique stress induced by the never-ending reality of working while others are playing. For example, while millions of people enjoy time off during holidays, these are the times theme park employees work the hardest. When other kids are out of school and able to travel for family visits, a park employee is tethered to their work location. Work schedules can routinely change, and hours are extended with very little notice based on park attendance, which can make childcare, transportation—and even eating—more of a challenge than the average guest might imagine.

There is another weird common behavior shared by tourists of both Hawaii and Walt Disney World that can wear down even the hardy: Super-fans can be super-difficult. In both instances, the folks who love the destination the most can be the most demanding and/or entitled. There seems to be an unspoken assumption that working at the "Happiest Place on Earth" should be its own reward, and pixie dust makes the job of serving them "fun." Occasionally this is true, but like any kind of show business, backstage feels a lot different than onstage. It was our belief that hula dancers and luau employees probably experienced the same thing—and they do. We were never under the impression it was going to feel the same as vacationing.

But moving to "The Islands" presented a different challenge if only by virtue of its wildly transitory population. Like Dorothy says after a few minutes in Munchkinland, "People come and go so quickly here." And, as a result, we found folks in general to be reluctant to engage either personally or professionally. Odds were you wouldn't be staying long, so why get too attached? We remained undeterred and enthusiastically optimistic about our decision to be residents of Maui and even had our home officially blessed by an official spiritual elder known as the *Kapuna*.

SAVED BY THE BANK

Everything involved with the move cost considerably more than originally budgeted—everything. From home inspections to quarantining our dog for a month (horrible), there seemed to be unlimited fees required to enter "island living."

After the sand settled, I sat whale-watching from our tiny, tiny beachfront condo, distracted by the calculating going on in my brain. The financial cushion of nine to twelve months had been wildly optimistic; the truth was we had about four. This made it hard for me to be serene in the moment.

We were to learn, immediately, that this was a common distraction among transplants from the mainland. People clucked and fussed about money incessantly, asking each other, "How are YOU making this work?" Most of the people we met were not rich retirees but average people with average jobs struggling to make ends meet. There is a common joke that everyone living in Hawaii has at least two of three licenses to be a driver, realtor and/or massage therapist. It can feel like everybody's on the hustle to pay for paradise.

Should one forget for a moment about the cost of anything, don't worry, the tourists are always there to remind you at every opportunity. A fun thing to do is hang out near the bread aisle at the local Safeway as travelers pick up a loaf and shriek. They'll run around the store in pairs, yelling out the prices of everything to each other in disbelief. "Seven dollars for a box of Cheez-its, Honey! Can you believe it?" "Look over here—six dollars for bread? Oh, my GAWD!"

After several weeks of trying to hide from John how worried I was becoming about money, I got one of the first calls on my first cellphone while walking on the beach. "There you are! We've been trying to find you," said a cheery voice with just the slightest southern twang. "This is Pam with Bank of America, and we want to talk to you about helping us become a 'most-admired' company for service." Our world can change in a twinkling of an eye.

Several months had passed since I'd met the representatives from Bank of America, and I'd forgotten all about the card in my wallet. They had tasked this lady with finding me in an age prior to Facebook or LinkedIn, and Disney was not in the habit of giving ex-employee contact information to potential clients.

"Can you be in Charlotte, North Carolina for a meeting on Monday morning?" (This was the Friday before.) "Of course," I said, not having any idea how or how long it would take to get there from Maui. I would get to know this thirteen-hour commute very well.

PUTTING THE CAMERA BACK TOGETHER

My first assignment outside Disney was a whopper and an honor: co-writing and delivering "The Bank of America Spirit" in 2001. Foundationally, my task would be the same: inspiring/ imploring thousands of hardworking banking associates around the country to see the customer experience with fresh eyes. I was needed to help make the case that "magical moments in banking" could and should be happening all the time, for customers and employees alike.

Admittedly this first flight out of the Disney nest brought on a lot of anxiety. The work I had done with visiting clients to the Disney Institute had been largely in theory; it had never been my responsibility to take it back home and implement our services at other companies. Would I actually be able to help guide a service culture-shift outside the cozy confines of the Disney campus? Even though I had the help of a lot of talented individuals, was this too big an assignment too soon? Had I bitten off more than I could chew?

Just as I was beginning to reach full-panic mode, a famous story about Walt Disney came to mind and provided me with comfort and inspiration. During his earliest days as a filmmaker, he wished to know every detail of how a moving picture camera worked. Not having his own, he borrowed one from his current employer for a weekend and proceeded to take it apart bit by bit. It would be a pretty good bet the boss had no idea this was happening. Soon, every piece of the camera was spread across the floor, and Walt had to figure out how to put it back together without the help of written instructions, photos, or YouTube. This is how he learned to operate and understand the mechanics of the camera to achieve magic on film.

My experience at Bank of America was very similar and had the same outcome. I created a process that made practical sense to me and, fortunately, much success and opportunity followed. I had figured out how to put the camera back together again.

In the project that lay before me, the service culture of Bank of America was the figurative camera, and a large variety of skilled hands joined mine to reassemble it again. In a quick and surreal life transition, I found myself in Charlotte, NC, shut in a room with a talented technical writer as she and I hashed out a training program in five days that would be known as "The Bank of America Spirit."[6]

Some coworkers on the project weren't sure how the extremely talented but left-brained technical writer and the

---

6 We wanted to call it "The Spirit to Serve," but Marriott already owned that title.

possibly talented but right-brained training designer would get along at first. It turned out to be the perfect marriage, and writing that program with Dorothy proved to be one of the easiest and most joyous professional efforts of my career.

While much of our work was and is proprietary, I can share that "The Bank of America Spirit" was the dawn of a new of way of *being* Bank of America in service to customers and coworkers. The culture shift was kicked off by a two-and-a-half hour presentation to be delivered to every bank employee all over the country. It was unapologetically theatrical and emotional and designed to engage the hearts of bank associates.

In the process of writing and implementing the initiative, I discovered/developed the "culture wheel" (pictured below) I still use for guiding organizations and individuals through the attainment of service "superpowers."

Essentially, we'll use this same process wheel as we master the ten skills of the service superhero (you).

STORY

Just as it is with individuals, organizations will always have a **foundational narrative**, which provides context for their behaviors. One of the components that made Disney's orientation for new hires so successful was its ability to marry the rich history of the company Walt had built with an invitation to join the narrative by making magical memories. I knew that employees liked contributing to a legacy, and I would come to learn that Bank of America associates had no idea they even had one. Nobody had focused on the company's story for a very long time, so the employees were, for the most part, completely unaware of what the company they worked for had achieved or what it had done for their country. There was a treasure trove to work with, and I felt it was imperative to share some of it in our presentation as a way of cementing our **intention**.

LANGUAGE

I immediately found a lot of nasty elements in bank vernacular, but the most curious (to me) was the incessant need to say, "Yeah, but we're bankers," or "Just remember we're bankers," or "We probably did that because, well, we're bankers." It was reflexive and rather like an annoying tick or a mantra. I wasn't sure if it was meant to be an apology, an excuse, or an alibi. Like most multinational companies, Bank of America had become a little clumsy about the way they spoke of themselves internally.

"Stop saying that!" I cajoled early on, and we set about redefining the current banking lexicon with words and terms more emotionally driven.

BEHAVIORS

The average bank associate had never considered the concept that they were **onstage** while they accomplished their daily tasks. In the past, being "nice" was never really a prerequisite for working in finance. Not that they didn't have behavioral guidelines—oh boy, did they: a thumping tome of a manual.

Neither was my project the bank's first swing at customer service initiatives. We would be facing a "been there—done that" attitude, and it would need to be candidly addressed. The best intuition I had was to avoid the paradigm of "We're going to *behave* differently," and go instead with "We're going to use what we already know about ourselves and our customers to *be* the best we've ever been."

Almost every bank associate could articulate *what* outstanding customer service looked like, but many had disconnected with the *why*.

RECOGNITION

Too many companies pull a bait 'n switch tactic regarding employee recognition. A majority of the time, an organization will communicate its most important values, only to reward a different set altogether at the fiscal year's end. "Service to our customers is what we value most," I'll hear the CEO proclaim from the podium, followed by "And now the award for who sold the most this year!"

Like Disney, Bank of America was going to have to enrich its overall narrative with current examples of excellence because any group (of anything) needs to constantly recognize whatever it wants more of. Lastly, we needed to get their employees to recognize the value that can come from exceeding expectations … in other words, what was in it for *them*.

PUTTING ON A SHOW

I cannot stress enough how many talented individuals had to come together and "brain bond" to make The Bank of America

Spirit the tremendous success it became. We trained facilitators, whom we called "Spirit Makers," from banking centers all over the country and dispatched them in groups of three along with a team coach (I was among the four) to convey the message by way of an extremely theatrical presentation.

Unlike other presentations on customer service they had seen, this was shamelessly emotionally charged and customized around the real-life stories of the facilitators on stage. We worked for weeks on their storytelling skills, and I even employed many of the improv techniques I had learned at Disney to make the presenters feel more comfortable onstage.

Among the heroes involved in the project, I have to pay special tribute to a gentleman by the name of Kent Parham. Kent is one of those Jack-of-all-trades who can seemingly do everything. Besides working as a leader in various capacities within the bank, he also staged many of the televised statewide Miss America Pageants on the side. Kent was fluent in Show Business.

The plan was to present the program/show in many dozens of separate locations, usually in local hotel ballrooms. I knew how much employees disliked such events from an earlier project with ExxonMobil—the last time I would ever present material I didn't have a hand in writing. I wanted to attempt something very different, and Kent was there to back me up on a unique suggestion.

"We keep referring to this program as a show," I said. "So, why don't we do it in theaters? Instead of doing tons of small presentations in tiny, individually rented meeting rooms, let's do it fewer times but way bigger!"

Kent knew where I was headed, and his experience with the televised pageants was instrumental in making it happen.

He created a fabulous (inexpensive and durable) set that could travel from city to city, as well as a detailed lighting plan for the local techs to follow.

To most bank associates, The Bank of America Spirit was a multimedia extravaganza, the like of which they had never seen or expected from their employer. We played a lot of huge (often famous) venues, including the Kodak Theater in Hollywood, where the Oscars were about to be held—that was a thrill. Best of all, the initiative was a huge success for the bank and my speaking/consulting business. Customer satisfaction scores soared, and for their efforts to improve the banking experience, Bank of America earned recognition across the industry. I was noted as "their consultant from Disney" in a piece by *Money* magazine.

Since then it has been my pleasure to work with great and varied organizations, from insurance companies to small town municipalities, and I owe much of it to marrying my narrative with two of the greatest brands in U.S. history: Bank of America and Disney. They opened a lot of doors, and I will forever be grateful. Any further examination of my resume would be beside the point and beneath our collective purpose.

Occasionally, we all have to "take the camera apart" and put it back together again in order to record our story. That's what the next part of this book is all about: how to take apart your own camera and put it back together again.

INTRODUCTION TO THE TEN SKILLS
OF THE SERVICE SUPERHERO

Let us begin by addressing the flying elephant in the room: Almost no one reading this book is working at a happy-go-lucky theme park, even if they actually are working at a theme park. In all candor, some of you may even hate your present jobs, and I'd wager that practically all of you feel undervalued or undercompensated.

This first thing to remember is how much you've forgotten. I rarely meet a service professional who is truly in touch with the impact their work has on others. Presently, there is an individual who has benefited and continues to benefit as a result of your service excellence. When was the last time you stopped to consider the end results of your service performance? Have you ever?

For many, providing excellent service isn't about serving food or selling balloons. It can also be about soothing a frantic pet owner or having the right words to say on the other end of a suicide prevention call. Good service can include getting passengers safely off a plane, or calming a patient as they're about to go into surgery. The experiences I share here and the examples given through the lens of an entertainment enterprise are not meant to trivialize any other specific line of work. I'm going to assume costumed characters and rollercoasters are not part of your "show" and wish to be respectful of your challenges.

No matter what your specific role in your service life is— delivering pizzas or delivering babies—you are probably being overwhelmed by tasks at this very moment. **Task** is the great foe of employee engagement, and tasks rarely disappear— in fact, they have a way of growing and multiplying. Most service professionals begin their jobs or careers with the best of intentions only to be thrown off course by a tidal wave of tasks. Pretty soon we can forget the job altogether and singularly serve the task to survive.

Isn't it time to take some of your power back and realize you either have to drive your circumstances or let them drive you? While certain circumstances will always be beyond our control, I'm convinced our ability to steer our lives (professional and personal) is vastly underestimated.

There is a difference between one's task and one's job. At Disney we would emphasize that while there were hundreds of different tasks, everyone had the same job with the same intention: creating magical memories for their guests. Whatever line of work you, the reader, may be in, the same is true in your situation. You probably have many tasks, yet only one ultimate **intention**.

The first part of this book detailed my circuitous path to discovering the Ten Skills of the Service Superhero to provide context and make your quest a little easier. The following chapters will act more like a workbook, in that we deal with one skill at a time and relate it to your personal experience and application.

Like any power, super or otherwise, the skills necessary for developing it require discipline, dedication, and practice before you can become a "hero" in delivering the ultimate best of customer experiences. It begins by affirming that **an investment of yourself is an investment in yourself.**[7]

There is another reason investing **of** oneself has power: Excellence seeks and finds more excellence. This is why people who find joy and provide excellence in a company's mailroom are plucked out, while others loathe it and remain. Points of excellence will always find other points of excellence, regardless of class or station. Look around and you'll find living testaments of this principle everywhere.

---

7 That was almost the title of this book, *An Investment OF Yourself Is an Investment IN Yourself,* but my agents found it too abstract—they were probably right.

As we move forward, I suggest reading only one chapter a day for ten straight days, ideally. (The next chapter will require a little pen-to-paper action as we isolate and identify your intention, and it will take a longer investment of time than the rest.) As is true with any training, consistency is the most important element in developing skills. In becoming a service superhero, a little effort every day is more valuable than a tremendous effort one day a week.

The following chapters will examine one service super-skill at a time, anchored by a real-life example of that skill in practice. Try reading a chapter as early in the day as possible (maybe before work) then spending ten minutes contemplating its relevance to you. Write the title of the chapter somewhere in the book, look at it, let it go, and let your mind ponder. Doodle all over the book if you want to.

That's all there is to it! This effort will be enough to see an experiential difference.

My life has been graced with a lot of good fortune; so many childhood dreams have come true. On the first day of kindergarten, I told anyone who would listen that someday I would be an actor on television AND work for Disneyland. Both happened. Like most people, my **intention** defined my **process**, and that is what I aim to share with you now—a process that includes the **Ten Skills of the Service Superhero** (another excellent but rejected title for this book!), a system that is practical and actionable.

So many of my goals have been achieved or manifested through the power of service, including the speaking career I enjoy now. What was the most instrumental thing that prepared me for my journey of goal gathering? Losing everything and then learning how and why to be a terrific food server. That's when my "superpowers" were developed and what pointed me in the direction of my dreams.

My adventures have taught me that the only way to retain anything of real value is to keep giving it away. This is the reason I began to develop the Ten Skills of the Service Superhero and why I *need* to share them with you now.

THE TEN SKILLS
OF THE SERVICE
SUPERHERO

CHAPTER SEVEN
THE TEN SKILLS OF THE SERVICE SUPERHERO
#1. SERVING WITH INTENTION

"It is by a man's purposive choice that we judge his character—that is, not by *what* he does but what he does it *for*."

—*Aristotle*

THE PROSCENIUM

As chapter one makes abundantly clear: There's no business *but* show business. If this is true (and I believe it is) then we can think of our overall **intention** as the proscenium, or the frame, for our entire show—our **context**. We've chosen intention rather than **purpose** as our first skill because our intention informs our purpose. A single intention can serve a variety of purposes simultaneously, and a purpose is usually supported by an abundance of tasks.

As I alluded to earlier, the connection between task and intention was a major learning during the cross-utilization training for new-hires. Examination of excellence among the multitude of roles at Walt Disney World was an important part of preparation, and many of the tasks we learned were not pretty. We were specifically introduced to the grind of bathroom cleaning in different milieus all over property, which was just as imperative to the curriculum as other tasks.

We would be met at our appointed locations by stars of the departments that were hosting us for the day whose role it was to teach us and enlighten us about working life in their specific locations. I was aware we were interfacing with "ringers" to some degree and shown situations under the most positive point of view possible. Still, my experiences in cross-utilization training were invaluable as I constructed the "story-flow" of my training day.

THE PIZZA LADY

Of all the lessons and insights gleaned from my cross-utilization experiences, none influenced me more than my lunch shift with the Pizza Lady. Sadly, I have long since forgotten this wonderful woman's name, but in the romance of memory I recall her as "Mamie."

Mamie had spent most of the last nineteen years backstage at Tomorrowland in the Magic Kingdom making pizzas for one of the quick-service locations in the park. She was quite a character on many levels—mature (probably nearing seventy) and tiny, and she spoke with a deep-throated Southern drawl. Even though Mamie had good dental insurance, it had never occurred to her to have her missing front teeth replaced. Being in her company was a blast.

After learning the "magic" of cleaning hotel bathrooms and separating bed sheets, this task of making pizza with Mamie was a welcome respite. The task didn't appear to be difficult. The flattened pizza dough lay in a long line waiting for tomato sauce to be brushed on, a layer of cheese spread across it, and pepperoni tossed on top with a flair at the end. Frankly, it seemed like a lark, especially after my recent adventures in learning how a family can destroy a hotel room with a single delivery from room service.

The ever-present Mamie was watching on, arms folded, as I went about humming and tossing ingredients at the pizza dough. Humming and tossing, tossing and humming until Mamie could no longer quell an intervention. The kind woman put her hand on my shoulder and, with all the earnestness of a private nurse, counseled: "Huh-ny! Huuuh-ny, huuuuuh-ny. No way, uh uh, baby. See, if you don't get that cheese all over that pizza all even-like, it ain't gonna be *good show* for mah gueeeests."

In nineteen years, Mamie had never, in fact, interfaced with a paying guest—not once. And yet, this cast member never lost sight of the fact that her **task** was to prepare hundreds of pizzas during an average morning shift, but her **job** was to create a "good show" for thousands of people she would never meet. This was Mamie's contribution to the magical memories of *her* guests. No matter what we think we're doing, we all have to figuratively "get that cheese around the pizza all even-like," just like Mamie told me.

That day I learned the importance of always seeing the results of your service efforts through the lens of the customers' eyes as a way of bringing you back to intention, and I dedicated myself to the science of communicating this lesson to others. In fact, in large part, that is my intention. Now let's examine your intention.

START BY STARTING

"The power of decision is my own."
—*A Course in Miracles*
Lesson 152

At the start of my "SERVICE IS A SUPERPOWER!" seminars, I will often begin by asking various participants in the crowd what they do—or *think* they do—for a living. Almost without exception they fire-off their title or task but rarely articulate the intention or purpose of their jobs.

In a room of 500 healthcare professionals, for example, I'll query, "What do YOU do?" and invariably hear, "I'm an X-ray technician" or "I'm a nurse!" These are *job titles*. When the audience can tell that's not what I'm looking for, they move to yelling out specific tasks. "I help patients make appointments and do schedules" or "I draw blood!" … still not what I'm looking for. Almost never will I hear, "I heal people!" or "I'm in the business of healing."

It's the same thing no matter what manner of business, be it banks, insurance companies, or hamburger chains: "I'm a teller," "I'm a claims adjuster," "I take food orders." While all of these responses are factually correct, they are completely divorced from the emotional outcome of the services rendered. This is called **task-thinking**, and I'd bet everything in my wallet you've fallen victim to it at some point and may even be squandering you work-life away in it now.

Recall my earlier quote from Lee Cockerell about WIN, i.e., what's important now? What is important first is that you take control of your narrative by reconnecting with the emotional outcomes of your efforts, just as organizations must do to create cultural shifts back to their primary intention, or what I call their **foundational narrative**. Let's start with isolating and identifying your narrative.

WHAT DO YOU DO?

This is not a trick question, but as I've illustrated, most of us have a difficult time fully answering with clarity. Using myself as an example, I might be tempted to throw out my title: I am a public speaker and consultant. Or maybe my task: I give funny speeches about improving customer service. However, my intention is to be a catalyst for self-improvement through the power of service, so my core product is "inspirational fun."

Disneyland is an amusement park. It offers amazing rides and shows and sells premium-priced food items while creating life-long memories. Disney execs will be the first to tell you that they are in the business of creating and selling "happiness." It's even in the mission statement we used to teach new hires: "We create happiness by providing the finest entertainment for people of all ages—everywhere."

Looking at other examples, let's imagine you work the floor in a "big box" chain store like a Walmart, Target, or Sam's Club— what do you do? Your job title may be "salesperson" and your task to make it easier for shoppers to find and buy what they want/need. But what is the emotional component involved?

Value.

You're selling value and, in the process, improving your life by exceeding the expectations of others with grace and service. In this instance, value is your core product.

Let's look at another scenario.

Perhaps you sell drinks at a local pub. You're typically titled "bartender" and tasked with responsibly selling and serving alcoholic beverages. There are probably buckets full of other chores you're responsible for—among them, stocking the bar, cleaning it, inventory, keeping the ice clear of glass, and checking identification. What are you selling? Good times—fun. (Hopefully responsible fun, but fun nonetheless.)

Keeping a focus on what we're really selling at any given time helps to ground us in our personal foundational narratives—every great brand does this, and so should you. You too are a "brand."

I AM NOT A BRAND!

I have a very close friend I refer to as Nurse Nancy. I do this for primarily two reasons:

Her name is Nancy.

She's a nurse.

Nurse Nancy works very hard as a charge nurse at an extremely busy intensive care unit in the Orlando area and took slight umbrage with the concept of "being a brand" as she was painstakingly proofreading this manuscript. "I am NOT a brand," she pushed back. "I provide a service—as a *person!*" Not quite satisfied she'd made her point, her closing statement was, "Service is not transactional."

To a great many of you also, the idea of being thought of or referred to as a "brand" is possibly abhorrent. It may conjure a cold, impersonal image, similar to being likened to a box of cereal. To all of you and Nurse Nancy I would argue the following points:

Brands are intensely emotional and hardly impersonal. A brand relationship is the result of intention, actions, and expectations, and so are own relationships, whether work-related or otherwise. We engage with brands based on appearance, promise, and reputation, which the same cornerstones we consider when building personal relationships. Our personal brands help us communicate our narratives to others in an effort to create productive relationships—just like brands of toothpaste.

Service is transactional! Service is transactional in much the same way as gravity. You don't have to *believe* in gravity; it's a law, and a specific cause will always result in a non-negotiable effect. We might not be able to see the end result from our present perspective, but that doesn't negate the assured outcome. If I make the choice to jump out of a window, I accept the effect of that cause as irrefutable. Similarly, the action of providing a service is making a cause, and the absence of an effect (immediately perceivable or not) would be impossible. (An excellent service professional paid primarily in tips knows you don't judge your worth by single transactions: sometimes you're generously compensated, and sometimes you get stiffed.)

A good way to think about the wow-service moments we create is to step back to see how they string together to create narrative in our lives, the same way individual works of art tell a story if you see twenty-four of them every second, as you do when you watch celluloid film.

Consider how each frame of a cartoon is painstakingly created, one at a time. Dozens of artists and technicians have to join hands (along with tons of money) for many hours to complete just one frame of animation. While each frame is beautifully crafted, in and of itself, it doesn't tell a cohesive story—it takes thousands of those single pictures coming together to provide perspective and narrative. The power of our service practices can also be perceived better with some distance.

One service moment, even the best ones, doesn't come close to representing the entirety of your story.

SPEAKING YOUR INTENTION:
WHY IT'S CALLED "WALT DISNEY" WORLD

Since our intentions have to be articulated, we need to solidify the language we want to use to support them. How we speak of things reinforces how we think of things. This is one of the most important things I learned about building a work culture from my time at the Walt Disney Company (the official nomenclature).

During the years I was training the trainers, there was one legend I insisted on sharing to make the point that language supports intention. I say "legend" because, like many pieces of Disney folklore, the story has been told around the campfire for decades and is bound to contain embellishments—even my own. However, the tale is relevant to us as we begin to identify how we want to speak of what we're being/doing.

The official legend (per my interpretation) goes like this:

Soon after quietly (and rather sneakily) acquiring forty-five square miles of central Florida in order to build a project Walt dubbed EPCOT (**E**xperimental **P**rototype **C**ommunity **of** **T**omorrow), a tumor the size of a walnut was found in one of his lungs. This was 1966, when the prognosis for lung cancer was never good.

Walt had a lot to live for and had no intention of dying, reportedly quipping, "I'll have them freeze me and thaw me out in ten years to fix whatever they do to EPCOT." Whether he really said that or not, my guess is this is where the urban myth about Walt Disney being frozen has its roots.[8]

---

8 In truth, he is interred at Forest Lawn cemetery in L.A., even though there are people who, to this day, will not be dissuaded from science fiction and insist that his head is on ice in a vault somewhere.

After the removal of one lung, Walt found himself in the hospital practically across the street from his studio. While recuperating from the surgery, he was visited one evening by his older brother and business partner, Roy. Roy was the "money man" of the operation and navigated the morass of Disney's financial enterprises. The men had weathered good times and bad and shared a close (if sometimes tumultuous) brotherhood.

Upon entering the hospital room, he discovered Walt focusing intently at the ceiling in deep concentration. "Look at this," Walt whispered hoarsely while grabbing his brother's arm and pointing up at the ceiling. "We have to set this up [EPCOT] entirely different than in California," he continued. "I wanna put a lake in front of the Kingdom part to act as an opening curtain. Let's surround it with enough land so nobody can see in or out this time."

Roy soon realized that his brother had being using the time in bed to map out the Florida project on the ceiling tiles above his head and was now trying emphatically to articulate his vision of the property. The man had just had a lung removed, but the power of his intention was fortifying his ailing body.

Impressed by the passion and purpose of his brother's condition, Roy left the hospital confident enough to phone Walt's wife, Lillian, and report on his visit. "I think he's gonna make it, Lilly. If for meanness alone, he's damned and determined to drag us all to that God-forsaken swamp to build this 'EPCOT thing'—don't worry."

Walt Disney died the next morning.

The family had done an excellent job of keeping Walt's condition a secret, so his passing at the age of sixty-five on December 15, 1966 came as a shock to the world and almost all of his employees. There was speculation that the Florida project would be postponed indefinitely, but Roy Disney made it clear slowing down was not an option.

"Oh we're goin' in," he said. "But we're not calling this thing EPCOT," (he didn't get it) "and we're not calling it Disney World either," he proclaimed to a baffled executive board. "We're going to call it Walt Disney World for two reasons. The first is so that nobody ever forgets it was my brother who dragged us all into the amusement park business—kicking and screaming." (This was a fact.) "And reason two … I don't want us to ever become like Ford. Everybody can tell you what a Ford is, where you can buy one, how much they cost, but nobody knows a thing about Henry Ford anymore!"

He was correct. Ford had become a faceless brand with little to no connection with the hero of their narrative. The company was living product-to-product. The Disney brothers had always had loftier ideas about their legacy, evidenced by one of the most exhaustively complete archives of any entertainment company in history. (Unlike MGM or 20th Century Fox, who sold or burned most of their history, Disney kept EVERYTHING.)

This dedication to intention (plus lexicon) is one of the reasons the Disney legacy remains an important part of our global consciousness and is easily identified. And solidifying our own way of speaking about what we're doing can help us to bring *our* goals into attainable focus.

So, let's examine your brand narrative exactly as a Fortune 500 company would.

FORMALIZING YOUR INTENTION
WITH LANGUAGE

First, we solidify our intention with our core product. As I wrote earlier, my core product is "inspirational fun." Knowing this, I can begin to develop the language I will use to communicate my brand intention.

Many organizations will communicate their values during the training of new hires. Some companies live by these values religiously, while others never mention them again after orientation. I believe in the former tactic. Having values firmly in place can serve as a matrix for thinking and consistent communication within an organization. Think of all the different businesses and disciplines involved with the operation of a theme park that have to be able to communicate with each other.

Disney sells happiness by utilizing the values of SAFETY, COURTESY, SHOW and EFFICIENCY. These standards, used as a prioritized "matrix of thinking," as well as a common language, work in practicality in the following scenarios.

SAFETY: Most guests are familiar with the classic attraction "Pirates of the Caribbean," where people ride a waterway in small boats, slide down a waterfall, and interact with dozens of audio-animatronic swashbucklers before making a fiery escape— typically harmless fun. Using the aforementioned matrix of thinking that utilizes agreed-upon standards, we would know the guests' SAFETY would be priority one. Should the boat capsize at the bottom of the waterfall causing a patron to drown, there is virtually no service recovery for death. Therefore, any and all choices regarding a guest's experience on the pirate attraction (Disney doesn't have "rides," they have "attractions") have to make safety paramount.

COURTESY: Another scenario would be where the experience is safe and technically impressive with practically no wait-time at all. But this time, a cast member swears at you as you're trying to exit the boat—service recovery possible but very difficult. So, COURTESY is the next link in the chain.

SHOW: The third scenario would entail a trip through the attraction with a safe, courteous, and expeditious adventure where someone forgets to turn on the robotic pirates. The service recovery wouldn't be quite as tough, but nowadays that moment is likely to be broadcast globally via social media within minutes. So, yup, SHOW is the next service pillar to uphold.

EFFICIENCY: Our last example would be a safe, courteous, and dazzling show ... but there's a ninety-minute wait to get in. You might not like it, but you'll FORGIVE the situation if the other three standards are fully in place. EFFICIENCY is vitally important but, in this case, the easiest one of their four standards to recover from.

Incorporating this language consistency makes it possible for communication across all roles. What four standards of excellence does your personal brand incorporate? These are important to identify, as they will support your mission to present your core product.

The following page contains dozens of the words I find are used most often in corporate mission statements. Look them over, think of your core product and then select the four that most speak to your cause. After identifying your standards of excellence, go ahead and prioritize them in an order that serves both you and your customers, patients, or clients.

We've taken a look at Disney's standards, now what about

yours? Should a word come to your mind that isn't on this list, go ahead and use it.

Accuracy | Talent |
Safety | Showmanship | Courtesy Efficiency |
Productivity | Heritage | Hardware | Software | Skill
| Availability | Empowered | Responsibility | Honor |
Relationship | Service | Awareness | Charity | Presentation
| Humility | Entertain | Teamwork | Presence | Story |
Innovation | Cooperation | Leadership | Compatibility |
Investment | People | Competition | Prosperity | Product-
Excellence | Accountability | Respect | Purpose | Provide
| Ownership | Salesmanship | Narrative | Recognition |
Fun | Individuality | Helpful | Performance | Health |
Value | Constructive | Training | Communicate | Security
| Willingness | Humor | Delivery | History | Creativity |
Knowledge | Educate | Integrity | Compassion |
Market | Honesty | Diversity |
Inspire | Catalyst

In my case, considering the product is inspirational fun, the four words that jump out at me are: CATALYST, INSPIRE, SERVICE, FUN.

For the aforementioned bartender, the words might be: RESPONSIBILITY, PEOPLE, PRODUCT-EXCELLENCE, FUN.

The salesperson at the big-box store might go with: SAFETY, COURTESY, HELPFUL, PRODUCT-EXCELLENCE.

The more life-and-death scenarios of the suicide prevention call-center employee may choose: HEALTH, KNOWLEDGE, COMMUNICATE, INDIVIDUALITY.

Combining my core product with at least two of the selected

values/service standards, my intention statement is: "I utilize inspirational fun as a catalyst for service-excellence."

The bartender's intention: "I responsibly provide fun for people with the finest refreshments, anywhere."

For the salesperson: "I help people acquire excellent products in a consistently safe and courteous environment."

And for the person facilitating the prevention of self-harm: "I use my knowledge and training to protect the health of every individual, through communication and compassion."

Now I'd like you to try the same technique. Using the four circles below, select the four values or standards that speak to your core product.

Marrying these components together and using at least two of the selected key words, create YOUR intention statement below:

_____

_____

Write this down (in your own handwriting) and place it somewhere you'll see it frequently. Go beyond memorizing the intention statement you've just created—OWN IT; however, don't feel you need to announce it to the world. In fact, it might be wise to stop anybody else's opinion from interfering with your intention for a while—maybe quite a while.

You have just completed the majority of the written "grunt-work" required to attain the skills of the Service Superhero because now that we have a solidified intention, it will focus all the other skills to follow!

CHAPTER EIGHT:
THE TEN SKILLS OF THE SERVICE SUPERHERO
#2. SERVING WITH KNOWLEDGE

KNOWLEDGE IS POWER!

In the world of customer service, Nordstrom is in a rarified league of its own and sets the standard for excellence in the retail industry. No one else comes close to their scores for customer satisfaction and loyalty, and it is usually the first name I hear shouted out during my workshops when asked for a brand that represents consistent excellence—even if they've never shopped or even been in a Nordstrom store.

Nordstrom's service training is also legendary. They make clear that each employee is expected to have extensive product knowledge, as well as traditional skills associated with customer service.

"Product knowledge is power. Salespeople should know everything about the item—the raw materials, the cut, the fit, the previous versions, and so on, because it gives them credibility with the customer."
—Dr. Robert Spector & Patrick McCarthy,
The Nordstrom Way to Customer Service Excellence

Knowing what your product or service looks, sounds, smells, and feels like through your customer's eyes can be more important than what it looks like through your own. The extensive product knowledge of the typical Nordstrom employee is one of the tools that makes them so adept at "fitting" the customer with the perfect item.

At Disney, we were never allowed to say, "I don't know," when asked a question. The proper response was, "Let me find that out for you," or "Let's find that out together!" Thanks to the internet, social media, and easy access to trade publications, extensive product knowledge is easier than ever before to acquire—much of it for free.

My assumption is that the typical person seeking to hone the skills of the service superhero is already well aware that knowledge is power but, like most of us, not always sure how to find more of it. What you choose to learn is a matter of your own inclination, but here are some ways to make the mind fertile and ready for new growth.

Decide to learn about something about a subject you know nothing about.

Sometimes the best way to acquire new knowledge is to enthusiastically embrace the "opportunity of ignorance" (more about this in a moment). For example:

- Read a book about something you know virtually nothing about and may have only a passing interest in. It can be a completely random topic or something you've always wanted to know more about, but it shouldn't be obviously related to your job.
- Attempt to play an instrument, even if you're horrible at it.

- Watch a foreign movie with or without subtitles. Go see a play or theatrical production in your community.
- Ingest news from a source outside of your own country.
- Watch cartoons with a kid and look at them through their eyes.
- Go to a different church one week.
- Force yourself to listen to some music you have dismissed as "not for you."

You don't have to be good at any of these things. I once heard Marianne Williamson say that nobody has hobbies anymore because none of us can tolerate participating in things we can't "master" or be immediately brilliant at. I think she's right.

Decide to learn something more about a subject you already know a great deal about.

- Try to look at things you already love through a different point of view. The world is filled with know-it-alls, and sharing wisdom with them is easier than ever before.
- Look for current documentaries about your points of interest—content abounds these days. Social media can actually have a positive influence in this regard as you glean knowledge from people and groups that share your passion.
- Reconnect with friends who share a common passion.
- Go back and listen to some of your favorite music from the past and remember what you loved about it.
- Revisit one of your favorite books from the past—it will spark a memory.

Use one of the amazing apps available to learn a new language.

Nothing has wiped the cobwebs out of my brain better than beginning to learn a new language five years ago. Trust me, there are whole corridors of your mind you haven't visited since you were a kid when you were deciphering language and learning to talk. Doing this in adulthood is like calisthenics for the brain, and you'll be amazed at how quickly you feel a benefit.

Learn to play video games—especially if you're over forty.

I know this may sound weird, but besides the improvement of hand-eye coordination skills, video games will challenge you with new concepts of problem-solving. Not all video games are violent shoot'em up affairs. I suggest games like Minecraft, which offer the opportunity to "build" things, racing games, or "platform" games like most of the Nintendo titles.

OWNING OUR IGNORANCE

There are some skills one shouldn't even attempt to fake. Playing the violin comes to mind, so does heart surgery. Roller-skating is another thing that really cannot be approximated—you either can or you can't. (If you don't believe me, take a look at my embarrassing go of it in a 1981 movie called *Evilspeak*—not even clever editing can mask my complete ineptness.)

As "service heroes," you serve no one by pretending you know about products or customer needs. Not that you'll ever stop learning and evolving on either of these fundamentals, but it's best to be authentic about your current level of expertise. Nobody wants to be that wedding officiator feigning a personal relationship with a couple they have clearly never met. (This practice is even more uncomfortable at funerals.)

The good news is that there is great power in consciously acknowledging one's lack of proficiency and owning the opportunity that ignorance offers. Declaring what you don't know allows new thoughts to find a home. It is impossible to build a ship in a bottle until the bottle is empty.

At the beginning of my journey in food service, I learned that a reasonable amount of candor about my lack of experience was not a bad angle to have, as long as it was accompanied by gracious good intentions.

Learning a better way of accomplishing a specific task will often require "forgetting" comfortable, well-worn methods while "remembering" our core mission and service. Occasionally we have to let go of what we think we know to expand our perceptions. Fortunately, brilliant people seem to enjoy sharing what they know with those who show aptitude and a willingness to learn.

Always remember there can be a certain freedom in a degree of ignorance, as it comes with a lack of prejudices or bad habits. Remember: You can't build a ship in a bottle until it's empty.

IF I HAVE TO BREAK EVERY BONE IN YOUR …

A pivotal experience for me was being cast in a huge, full-scale production of the musical *Hello, Dolly!* just weeks from turning sixteen years old. I hadn't mentioned to my parents that I was interested, and a friend drove me the thirty miles to the next town to audition for the supporting role of seventeen-year-old Barnaby Tucker, a part usually portrayed by a youthful looking adult. Imagine my mother's surprise when the producers called to offer her son a job in a show with television celebrities minutes before I returned home from the audition to tell her I'd been.

There was just one tiny hitch: When the producers informed the well-known choreographer, Alex Plasschaert, they'd hired a "real kid" to play the role, he was none too happy about it. "I don't have the time or patience for kids," he reportedly wailed, "I wanted to use a guy over twenty-one from my dance class!" Alex was not the classic stereotype of a choreographer—think General Patton, only really, really graceful.

I had not been warned what kind of animal I was being put in a cage with as I jauntily bounced in for the first day of rehearsal, eager and ready to please. The outfit I chose was a contemporary creation of denim overalls, a yellow gingham shirt with the sleeves rolled-up, a white driving cap (Robert Redford wore one in *The Great Gatsby*, so they were quite trendy at the time), accompanied by ridiculously tall platform tennis shoes. It was as if the musical *Newsies* was set in the 1970s.

With a wary eye, the choreographer queried, "Do you *dance?*" in a tone just short of a groan and more than a hint of contempt. I spritely responded, "Well, I've danced in five musicals already, but I've never had any formal training, Sir. I've just sort of faked it, I guess." This answer was both accurate and unsatisfactory for Mr. Plasschaert.

"Let's make an assessment then," he challenged and taught me a short set of moves to see what he was dealing with. He made three quick observations:

I had, indeed, *not* been taught how to dance.

I *could* be taught how to dance.

I had an earnestness and wide-eyed willingness to work that made it nearly impossible for him to be mean to me.

With a combat-weary look on his face, he said, "Well, I'm going to teach you to dance this part, young man. I'm going to teach you to dance this part if I have to break every bone in your little adolescent body in the process." (People still got away with talking that way to kids in the seventies.)

He remained the strict taskmaster, but he took me on in the way someone brings home a puppy they don't really want but know they're gonna get attached to, and resistance is useless. In return, his approval was vitally important to me, and I worked tirelessly at the fundamentals he was bothering to share with me.

I wasn't (and still am not) a quick study with dance. Unlike learning lines of dialogue, picking up dance routines has always required much, much more effort from me than most people. Once I do learn choreography, however, I seem to remember it for the rest of my life, perhaps a testament to how hard I worked to learn it in the first place. Yet my dance mentor, aware I was spending hours before and after rehearsal (how did I get through high school?), showed an unexpected amount of patience as I followed his lessons.

Fortunately, the time and effort he and I had to exert turned out to be worth it for both of us because the show was a big success and, thankfully, so was I. In the process, Alex Plasschaert taught me the two most important things about acquiring new knowledge:

First, never try to run before you can walk, no matter how anxious you are to succeed. There are very few shortcuts in life, and learning the basics of your field will serve you forever. As legendary dancer Andre De Shields said recently, as he accepted his Tony Award at the age of seventy-two: "Slowly is the fastest way to get to where you want to be." He's right; being a "late bloomer" is not the worst thing to be.

Second, show that you're teachable. No one will want to mentor you unless you make it clear you know you need mentoring. (This second one has been harder for me to remember.)

Years later, I realized why he eased up and became an advocate for my success—I had checked all of my attitude at the door and was authentically willing. Owning up to my ignorance paid off greatly, and he'd be happy to know I actually made a few bucks dancing professionally—if just a few.

YOU DON'T GET PAID FOR WORKING

"People are not paid according to what they are worth but according to their consciousness of specific money."
—Dr. Robert Bitzer, *The Essays of Robert Bitzer*

Many years ago, I use to attend a church in Hollywood founded by Dr. Robert Bitzer, a brilliant man who wrote many books on the "Science of Mind." He was well into his eighties by the time I came to know of him, and he spoke in a deliberate, raspy voice but with conviction. One Sunday he rose from his seat, marched briskly to the lectern, and whispered into the microphone in his Carolina drawl as if he were revealing a magnificent secret: "Nobody gets paid for working … they get paid for *knowing*." I remember thinking at the time, *What?*

For years this assertion seemed more than a little abstract to me, but Dr. Bitzer was, as per usual, right on the money. In fact, nobody *does* get paid by virtue of simply how hard they work, they get paid by virtue of how they think and what they think about.

Evidence of this axiom certainly abounded at Disney. For example, the performers who provided witty improvisational comedy at Pleasure Island made a much more comfortable living than those mowing lawns at the resort's golf courses. This is in no way meant to imply a lack of value (or profitability) in hard work, but there is a difference between working hard and working *smart*.

Toil and treasure have a complicated relationship. Take food service for example, as there is no more hard, honest labor or a more admirable skill than waiting tables, but the food servers at the Rainbow Room in Manhattan aren't working harder or sweating more than employees at the Waffle House (in fact, the latter may be a much harder gig). Both service providers may utilize the same physical skills, but the workplace they find themselves in will be dictated by a particular skill set involving consciousness. "As a man thinketh, so is he."

In short, the more we know, the more we're worth; therefore, knowing our own worth is infinitely more valuable than committing facts to memory. Ultimately, life is not an episode of *Jeopardy!*

THE SOLUTION HAS ALREADY BEEN INVENTED

Is anything truly invented anymore? Was anything ever really invented? It seems to me that "invention" is the discovery or definition of already-present truths; Benjamin Franklin didn't invent electricity, he discovered a way to use it. Invention is always collaborative, too. Walt Disney didn't invent animation, but he redefined it using the discoveries of countless previous artists who had already contributed to the collective knowledge of the craft.

Once someone uploads something to cyberspace, it is there forever, lying in wait, accessible to anyone with the persistence to find it. The collective mind we share, I'm convinced, works in exactly the same way. The instant anything is posted on the internet, it belongs to anyone, whether they're aware or even want to be aware of it or not. There is one collective-cyber mind (the internet) with an infinite amount of individual portals (computer devices). In turn, there are a lot of brains out there but only one shared mind. Our meditations, conscious or not, work like search engines, accessing shared knowledge—some of which you've provided.

Think of the comfort this concept offers as we set about amassing knowledge as power. If someone has ever figured out how to solve the problem you perceive—at any time or place—then you have access to that solution. It's a matter of finding.

You can tell what sites your brain is "browsing" by what you're attracting in your life. You will intersect with like-minded people. I took it as a great sign in my speaking career when I kept running into and meeting with individuals more successful than myself in that industry: It meant I was thinking like them and as them! (This is just one of the reasons you should always have a few friends way smarter than you—trust me, I've been employing this practice since kindergarten.) Whose head are you sharing when you're at work?

When you find yourself at a disadvantage based on your knowledge or expertise, tell yourself, "Somebody has learned how to handle this—that means the solution exists and is accessible to me." There is a peace (however slight) that can come from realizing problem-solving is more a matter of discovery and acceptance rather than invention.

"The mind contains all knowledge. It is the potential ultimate of all things. To it, all things are possible."
—Ernest Holmes, *The Science of Mind*

CHAPTER NINE:
THE TEN SKILLS OF THE SERVICE SUPERHERO
#3. SERVING WITH VISION

*"Change the way you look at things and the things
you look at will change."*
—Dr. Wayne Dyer, *The Power of Intention*

A BOOK AND ITS COVER

I am convinced that whoever came up with the phrase, "You can't judge a book by its cover," was someone just making an excuse for being unobservant. Frankly, there is an abundance of information on the cover of a book—there may not be the entire plot or enough indication of the quality if the writing, but evidence of intention and taste are all over the place. The selected color scheme, the quality of the author's photograph, the publishing company, the notes on the inside flap provide plenty of clues about what the readers can expect.

The first sense we use to establish a relationship with a person (unless they're extremely loud or aromatically challenged) is sight. How we perceive what we're seeing is based on past experience, still our vision usually provides the context for the rest of our senses. As shallow as it may sound, our visual attraction motivates most of our choices. Even when something sounds, smells, and tastes terrific, if we find it visually unappealing, we're likely to take a pass (hence my issue with creamed corn).

Disney has always been known for attention to beauty and cleanliness at their parks and resorts. They know every detail "speaks" in the experiences they prov but the first and most important question is "What's it going to *look* like?"

THE MOST EXPENSIVE COKE CUP IN HISTORY

There are those who walk among us with truly biblical amounts of disposable income, and Disney is happy to take some of it to create customized events, designed to make their individual dreams come true.

Most people are surprised to learn how much business goes on after hours in the parks, from large corporate events to small but elaborate offerings for very small, wealthy families. (One time we did an entire parade for one very rich family!) Various attractions can be rented for short periods during these events, and the Tower of Terror at Disney's Hollywood Studios is one such available offering (they don't come cheap, so save up).

The tallest point at Walt Disney World is not the spire of Cinderella Castle, but the 199-feet tall Tower of Terror.[9] I was working at Disney/MGM the year they opened the Sunset Boulevard expansion featuring the tower as its major draw at the end of the street. The attraction is housed in what appears to be a 1930s' Hollywood hotel, still smoldering from being struck by lightning on the thirteenth floor.

---

9 Artist renderings show a weather vane capping off the building—sadly, this had to be scrapped because it would have put the structure at over 200 feet, requiring a red light for air traffic.

To this day, it is still one of the most impressive (and expensive) attractions you'll ever lay eyes on. Guests climb aboard seated elevators, which take them on a surreal trip through "The Twilight Zone" and into an elevator shaft, slamming them up and down the hotel's thirteen floors several times in quick succession. It's both horrifying and delightful. The attraction is also a perfect representation of Disney's attention to detail. The vintage furnishings are authentic, while the many of the books in the library are first addition relics. Guests find themselves immersed in light and sound, while guided through a heavily themed narrative.

Since I portrayed the movie mogul who ran the studio, I would often earn overtime by hosting these custom trips through the ride. The routine was to meet the group at the front gate and lead them, with great flourish, on a walking tour through the park and into the ride. I was to stay in character as I hosted their journey, which usually climaxed with a cocktail party at the end of their visit to the attraction.

One night, the park was rented for a fantastically vulgar wedding with all the trimmings, including an hour with exclusive access to the ride. Money was clearly not an object—all of the ride vehicles from the Great Movie Ride had been removed so the wedding could be held in Munchkinland from *The Wizard of Oz*. But the bride, not wanting the children to be bored while she was having photographs taken, rented the Tower of Terror for an hour to entertain them—I came with the package.

As I was leading the group down the façade of Sunset Boulevard, as if I were Willy Wonka dragging kids through the chocolate factory, I couldn't help but notice the group's chaperone snapping her fingers above her head to get my attention. Edging my way to the rear, I heard, "The cup, the cuuup," emanating from her in a low growl. I had no idea what she was talking about until I turned around and noticed a soft-drink cup had been left next to the "Hollywood Tower Hotel" sign. It was one piece of trash, probably missed by a custodian hurriedly cleaning between the park's closure and the start of the event. That soft drink cup costs the company about three cents to make, but that's all it took to pull focus from a $140 million attraction and cost a partial refund of thousands of dollars: $140 million to build—3 cents to destroy.

Everything speaks, and the volume at which is speaks is often dictated by the smallest things.

IT WILL NEVER LOOK THE SAME AGAIN

I will never forget the first time I saw the disembodied head of Mickey Mouse on a hook, and neither would you. It feels shockingly eerie and wrong somehow. Without the "animating" from the performers, the sculpted heads of the costume characters are strangely lifeless. The same is true when the audio-animatronic figures are turned off and all the lights are on.

Operating every day for at least twelve continuous hours takes a physical toll on these figures, and it's quite visible if you see them from two inches away, as I have. I used to interact with the robotics in the Great Movie Ride for special events, so I got to see them up close and personal too. You know what? They never looked the same to me again.

No matter where you work, eventually you will "see the robots with the lights on," after which it becomes increasingly difficult to remember what things look like through your customers' eyes. And yet, it's imperative you do remember, not only for the benefit of your customers but also the benefit of your service mindset as well.

Sharing or sampling the experience you offer your clients will help you to see things afresh—for better or worse. Many of us have a way of tuning out what we don't wish to see or face, as if we put gauze over our eyes for a softer picture. Looking at a situation through the eyes of another is like turning the lights on inside of your "ride."

Think of the times you've been blissfully unaware of how untidy your home is until someone stops by unexpectedly; suddenly, you notice the results of every domestic chore you've put off for another day. Our friends with small children are completely numb to the fact their house looks like a cyclone swept through until other adults enter the dwelling. Like popping a balloon, your personal illusion is shattered when shared with another pair of eyes.

How many times have you quickly run into the supermarket, encountered an acquaintance then instantly thought, "Oh my God, I look terrible"? You just saw yourself the way you think other people see you. This is why I strongly recommend that you patronize the place you work (when possible) and bring family. Wear the clothing you sell, eat with your family in the restaurant you work at, and use the products you provide. This simple act can be a valuable tool for reconnecting with both the customers' vision of your service, as well as your employer's **foundational narrative** we spoke of earlier (the organization's story that you're helping to move along as a "character" in their living legacy).

WE MUST SERVE THE AVATAR!

Serving with vision also means looking into the future and anticipating needs or new opportunities. Those of us who dedicate our efforts to the customer experience can no longer ignore the "virtual" truth that we now have to excel at serving "virtual" clients too. Our customers' online avatars have come to expect the same level of service as their real-life counterparts.

It's been my good fortune to be a member of the same chain of health clubs (now known as L.A. Fitness) for over thirty years. In that time, each generation has brought its own spin to the strut-sweat-and-flex routine without too much deviation.

Until recently.

There is a new component of a young man's workout that never used to exist, a ritual now firmly entrenched into the gym-culture. I've named this dedicated and earnest exercise the "pose-and-publish," which is an astonishing development whereby, at the end of one's workout, selfies are taken in the mirror to record physical progress and then globally published. This behavior is taken very seriously and usually requires the mastering of a sultry, pouty look while flexing. This action is often followed up in the sauna, where their "followers" are treated to a live flex-chat while the gym enthusiasts talk about themselves and what they're going to eat next. Doing something but not sharing it on social media is a wasted effort. If a tree falls in the forest and nobody tweets about it, did it really happen?

We need to realize that offering the ultimate in customer experiences will require simultaneously **serving the customers' virtual lives, as well as their real ones**. The client's avatar must now be considered an integral part of the brand relationship and, as such, a member of the family to be served and indulged. So, how do we exceed the expectations of these new virtual customers and gain their loyalty? Well, if our core values are Safety, Courtesy, Showmanship, and Efficiency for our physical customers, the same should hold true for our digital patrons. We facilitate their existence, engage them as "costars" in the show and make them part of the experience.

The leading brands in customer service will be those that understand they must become **partners in personal publishing**. When my avatar virtually purchases tickets to the latest superhero movie, I'll expect to see Chris Evans as a Marvel character flying my CGI presence on his back through the world of Facebook as a way of saying "thank you."

But we have to be careful with this new genie-out-of-the-bottle. Deliver a bad customer experience and my social media imprint might chew you out so that I don't have to do it in person. Want to sell me a car? Talk to my avatar first! Want me to buy a new suit from your virtual department store? Well, show me how it would look on my digital alter ego! In the future, service will continue to be a superpower regardless of the "dimension" we're delivering it in.

BEING IN COSTUME

At the risk of sounding like one of those "You kids get off of my lawn" old men, your look is critical to anyone who works in the world of in-person service. It might even be critical for those of you who don't.

In short, kids, you have to look clean and sharp all the time. No matter your personal style, stay honestly committed to it but always, always LOOK CLEAN! The reasons for looking "ready" for your customers are obvious and don't need to be explored here in any depth. So, rather than talk about how your appearance makes clients and coworkers feel, let's examine how it makes YOU feel.

I have few criticisms of the intricate operations of Disney's theme parks (and mention even fewer), but a decision made about clothing a few years back has had, I believe, an unintended effect on service. For the first few decades the parks were in existence, a cast member's day would begin by picking up their costume (no "uniforms," only "costumes." Language, remember?) at a centralized location. This was a costly, time-consuming process, but it ensured every cast member looked consistently fresh, pressed and Disneyfied. Then, towards the end of the Eisner era, someone came up with idea of "cast-zooming." This was a new strategy allowing cast members to "zoom" in and out of work by laundering their own costumes. Of course, nearly everybody wanted to zoom, which was the idea all along.

This decision has saved the company untold millions of dollars but has come at a price. First, and the most obvious to predict, the cast members never looked quite as "show ready" once the company was no longer in charge of daily costume maintenance. It is fair to say that not all employees shared the same level of hygiene or laundering skills, resulting in an increasingly inconsistent personal appearance.

Second, the tourists do not like running into costumed cast members outside the environs of the resort. It makes the clothes look (and feel) less like costumes and more like uniforms, which they were never supposed to become. Whether we realize it or not, we're all "in costume" at work, no matter where that work happens to take place.[10]

---

10 Case in point. During a break writing this chapter, I met friends at a Chevy's restaurant. Upon entering, I saw four Disney cast members from the monorail sipping margaritas—it doesn't look good.

HOME SERVICE

There have been three separate times in my life I have left working for a large corporate entity and set about being self-employed. The first two attempts, I found myself struggling to create a consistent work structure, and I would return to the corporate world after floundering for a couple of years. The third time, I was determined to do things differently and it began with my "look."

The years I worked from home in Hawaii, I wore swimming trunks while puttering in my office. The year we spent in Palm Desert found me also donning swim trunks on a daily basis. What I learned was when you're constantly costumed for swimming you spend an inordinate amount of time in pools—when you're not catching up on a video game.

As corny as it sounds, I now get up every day and dress like something great is going to happen. I realize this means different things to different people, but for me it means putting on a shirt and tie (occasionally even a jacket) as I work in and around my home. When you're going to the beach, you dress for the beach; the same should be true for success. Besides, when we "look ready," we tend to go places and do things we might not otherwise feel confident enough to try. For example, you're much more likely to introduce yourself to a potential mentor if you feel like you look great.

Dressing "professionally" while working from home also sends a message to yourself and others that you're ready NOW. Which is a tidy transition into our next service skill.

CHAPTER TEN:
THE TEN SKILLS OF THE SERVICE SUPERHERO
#4. SERVING WITH PRESENCE

"Nothing has happened in the past; it happened in the Now. Nothing will ever happen in the future; it will happen in the Now."
—Eckhart Tolle, *The Power of Now*

HOW NOW, MR. JONES?

As you could probably predict, among the many thousands of personalities I encountered while working in the parks, some could be less than pleasant. Occasionally, some were, in fact, a nightmare. The most difficult audience to please can be the people who show up many times a year (or month) with higher and more specific expectations than the average tourist. At some point these expectations transcend into demands, then those demands become entitlements. Most of our regulars were lovely (many I still keep in touch with), but just as there are "good patients" and "bad patients," some of our customers would have had trouble earning gold stars for their behavior as guests.

Whenever I look back on some the toughest guest interactions, "Mr. Jones" comes to mind. I used to call him Mr. Jones because I didn't want to reveal his real name; now I call him Mr. Jones because I can't recall his name.

I didn't like Mr. Jones—there, I said it. Mr. Jones had a unique talent for rubbing me the wrong way. Besides having the nasty habit of reminding me how wealthy he was every five minutes, I found him to be arrogant, loud, demanding and, quite frankly, mean. Unfortunately for me, Mr. Jones was totally unaware of my feelings and enjoyed being in my company a great deal.

On a regular basis I would be "fetched" to show him a good time by driving him around the park in an old white car Walt drove around Disneyland in and used for the opening of Disneyland in 1955. It was a 1908 Oldsmobile, refurbished and retooled as electric, and I considered it a great privilege to be one of only two people allowed to drive it inside the park for years. In turn, Mr. Jones considered it a great privilege to have me drive him around the park for hours so he could wave at people, act important, and bark orders at me in a loud voice. I honestly felt guilty about how much I grew to dislike this person.

One day I was summoned to tote Mr. Jones and his (much more gracious) wife around in the white car at a time when I was not particularly in the mood for the challenge. Still, my job was to make magic for people, whether I found them likable or not, so I put on my best Disney attitude and gamely escorted the Jones' around like VIPs. After a few minutes, Mrs. Jones said to me, "Isn't this great for you! You get to come out here and have all this fun and you actually get paid to do it!" Without missing a beat, Mr. Jones snorted, "Ha! Honey, he doesn't get paid very much." And, with that, my tolerance for him *and* his condescending buffoonery was over.

Pulling the car briskly to the curb, I invited the Joneses out of the car, right in the middle of the park. This was unusual, but they acquiesced, probably assuming I'd been called away somehow. Just as they exited the vehicle and I was about to hit the pedal and scram, Mrs. Jones stopped me abruptly. "Wait," she pleaded, just as lovely as she could be, "I want to get a picture of you two men together before we go!"

I did not want to have my picture taken with Mr. Jones, not one little bit. However, I remembered my own lessons on the power of service, put on my most Disneyfied face and smiled through gritted teeth as she took the photo. Then I proceeded to go backstage and go on a completely and utterly self-righteous rant. "Why do we do that for him?" I seethed. "People spend years saving up to come here, and we don't do that for them, but he shows up and snaps his fingers and we're all supposed to ask how high he'd like us to jump." I wasn't nearly finished. "Don't ask me to drive him around again, he's yelled and ordered me around for the last time!" I was finished being Mr. Jones' personal jester at Disney.

Until about three months later.

"He's here and he's looking for you," said one of the VIP guides in red plaid. "He's been looking for you everywhere; he wants you to drive him around in the car." Remembering my resolve from our last encounter, I said something that had never come out of my mouth when requested to serve a Disney guest: "Nope." The look of panic on the guide's face told me he had not anticipated this response. "Yeah, but, I mean he's here and …" This time I didn't even verbalize my intention, I simply and slowly shook my head as if to say, "No way."

This was strange and unusual behavior for someone who had recently received the "Spirit of Disney Award" for service, but I would not be deterred. I bewildered everyone more by instructing random street performers to get into the car.

"See?" I declared with a sweep of my arms. "No room for Mr. Jones today."

The signal was given to open the large parade gate that allowed me to drive onto the stage. "Not today," I murmured under my breath as we rolled in with a flourish. Mr. Jones, whom I spotted out of the corner of my eye, was hustling breathlessly toward us with something in his hand, yelling, "HEY, YOU. HEY, YOOOUUU!" at the top of his lungs. This was the typical timbre of his voice, yet he looked considerably thinner than our last encounter. "Look at this, LOOK AT THIS!" he barked, waving a picture in my face.

"See this?" he hollered. "This is the picture my wife took of me and you the last time I was here. We didn't know how sick I was. Right after that, I ended up at Cedars-Sinai having surgery for cancer." He didn't tell me what type, and I didn't ask as he continued. "It was a real tough go—chemo, radiation, the whole deal." Then for the first time he spoke softly, "My wife brought this picture of us together to the hospital and said, 'when you get out of here, we're gonna go right back there, get back in that car with that young man, and we're going to pretend that none of this ever happened.'"

Silence. Beat … beat. Finally I said, "Okay, everybody, better get out of the car so Mr. Jones can get in."

I didn't know Mr. Jones, not really, and yet I had cast him as the villain of my show. My ego had no business complicating my intention, but I had let it. From that day forward, I seared the lesson into my brain: We don't know where people have come from, and we have no idea where they're going. The only thing we're sharing is NOW, that's it—that's all we've got.

Every one of those "now-moments" we facilitate helps to

define what we are willing to BE, not what we're willing to DO—that's entirely different. It's not what we're doing that counts; it's what we're *being*. People will forgive a mistake in service if the server is *being* sincere in his or her effort to please. A waiter may have no control over how long patrons have to wait for their order to be ready, but a skilled server knows a multitude of ways of being gracious enough to rescue a customer experience.

Conversely, we've all had restaurant experiences that fundamentally meet our needs in a perfunctory manner. We get seated at a table, a server takes our order, the meal or beverage comes as ordered and in a reasonable amount of time, the check comes, we pay, we go … but we might not come back. Each of those tasks can be completed and still leave a customer with a cold experience. No one expects (or wants) to become best friends with everybody who serves them, but they do want to feel you're being **authentically present** in the interaction you're sharing.

Remember the previous metaphor of viewing our service careers as one very long animated film unfolding one expertly crafted frame at a time. In and of themselves, each frame of animation is a beautiful piece of artwork created by many hands, over many hours of toil, and yet none individually tells a story or move a narrative along. You have to see twenty-four of those pictures a second rolling past your eyes to perceive action. The same is true of the myriad of service moments we create. One at a time, they may be perfect and complete, but they never convey the whole story arc. It takes time and perspective to perceive movement and change—the same will be true as you strengthen your service superpowers. It takes distance to recognize progress.

The only thing we can have any influence over is NOW. There may be days when it feels like you have to complete twenty-four "frames" a second just to maintain status quo, much less exceed expectations. Never waste a single moment or "frame"—our service to others helps define us and will always be recognized at some point, in some fashion, whether we're cognizant of it or not.

BUT I DON'T LIKE (THIS) NOW!

You may be saying, "But Louie, I hate the job I have—it's hard to enjoy *now* when you're miserable!" Fair enough, what do you do if you're unhappy at your present location?

First of all, ask yourself: Am I over this job, or is this job over me? Is your place of employment inadequate because it's an awful place in general, or is it wrong for you? Could you do better with your present skill set at a similar organization? Is everyone being treated poorly, or do you feel especially unsettled?

The reason to pose these questions is that you may find it is your wish/goal to move on but you're not brave enough to leave your present situation. In this case, some of us have a way of turning our present situation into such an untenable environment that it finally kicks us into our next episode. If all you're noticing at work is what's wrong, when you used to notice primarily what was right, that is a good indication you're "finished with that show." Don't let a good experience deteriorate into discontent just to force yourself out the door.

Fortunately, I have never had a problem keeping a job— except this one time when a stage manager and I developed an acrimonious relationship that, to this day, I don't quite understand, but we were "oil and water" as they say. Ultimately, this led to my being "let go" in an unnecessarily nasty fashion. Making things worse, there were four weeks left on the contract, and I was tasked with training my replacement.

Suddenly I found myself with a choice of how to react, not terribly different than the choice I was faced with as I entered life as a food server. The choice was between grace and contempt; thankfully, I was centered enough to choose the former. In fact, I "killed it with kindness," as my mother used to say. In short, I used gratitude as a power and it worked. Should you find yourself in a situation like this, I highly recommend this move because it's the best choice for your well-being and it totally unnerves the person/people who fired you—they can't stand it, and it's fabulous!

The more graciously I behaved, the worse my manager felt and the worse his managers felt about letting him do it, and this only served to embolden my stance. Was it an act? You know, at first, it *was* a performance. And then it actually started to feel good being able to "close-out" in that fashion. It may have been a complete coincidence or a result of my actions, but after that gig ended, I only went three days without a job.

APPRECIATING NOW WHILE WE HAVE IT

There are basically two kinds of people one meets while traveling for business: Those who pull out pictures of children, and those (like myself) who pull out pictures of pets. Grandparents and we "dog people" are particularly anxious to thrust pictures into strangers' faces. I've often wondered if it's the knowledge of how brief these special relationships are that allows us to appreciate how precious each second is.

The world is filled with other such triggers. Each of us must find our own "grounding triggers," i.e., those things in life that bring us back into the "now." For some, it's looking at sunsets.

For others, it can be music, food, or even exercise that brings us back into the glory of present-thinking. For me, it's the shower!

A lot of us begin our day by hosing ourselves down in the shower before we interact with another soul. This is a great way to launch your day in "now thinking" if, like me, you love a shower and have never taken it for granted. I stand there and marvel at the splendor of it all—the magical comfort that comes from a simple turn of a knob. It is literally flowing abundance falling wastefully upon you—and it's warm, ahhh. The luxury of it is rarely lost on me and the sensation often roots me in appreciation for the rest of that day's "episode" of my story. Find the grounding trigger that launches your day with the appreciation of "now."

CHAPTER ELEVEN:
THE TEN SKILLS OF THE SERVICE SUPERHERO
#5. SERVING WITH LISTENING

"Listening is a master skill for personal and professional greatness."
—Robin S. Sharma, *The Monk Who Sold His Ferrari*

Listening is a skill to be mastered, like any other behavior of the service superhero, and you may be surprised how many of us find this one to be the toughest. Some of it comes from our insatiable need to be right all the time, but some of the struggle comes with our discomfort with silence in general. The greatest comedians and improv artists in the world are those who have the confidence to use silence as a tool—so must superheroes in service.

Passivity-as-strength is a concept completely beyond the grasp of most Americans, unless we add "aggressive" to the phrase. However, as any martial-arts expert will tell you, **not doing** can pack an even greater punch than **doing** in certain circumstances. The art of "not doing" requires we learn how to actually STOP applying our personal will, in order to simply let things happen or reveal themselves to us.

We were never taught the strength of stillness in our school curriculum, and most of us either don't know how to achieve stillness or aren't comfortable with stillness when we achieve it. In Western culture, "active listening" usually means thinking about what you're going to say before the other person stops talking. In short, we just don't know how to shut up and listen.

Being listened to can be very satisfying for our customers. How many times have you found yourself not being able to get a word in edgewise while trying to explain the reason you called to speak to a service representative? It's not the representatives' fault; they're usually trying to solve your problem as quickly as possible. Or there are other occasions when the call center employee is being heavily monitored for efficiency. In fact, most often the call center employees we're speaking to are under the gun of a timer. This is how we find ourselves in "Mr. Jones situations," where we attempt to cut-to-the-chase by predetermining the outcomes based on a few faulty clues. If you find yourself trying to finish your customers' sentences as they speak, you're guilty of **bad listening for good intentions**.

But what does the term "not doing" really mean anyway?

WATSU MATTER YOU?

While living in Hawaii, I was exposed to several new spiritual exercises and techniques that I might not have encountered otherwise. Among the most fascinating and exotic of these experiences was my session in a Watsu pool. What's a Watsu, you may ask? Besides being an irresistible temptation for alliteration, Watsu is a form of "passive aquatic therapy" whereby a participant is guided by a practitioner (or therapist) who gently cradles and swirls them about in a pool of warm salt water. Small flotation tubes are utilized to suspend you in warm weightlessness, astonishingly, without water getting up your nose! Some people claim to have used the process as a sort of "rebirthing" session, allowing them to reach a very quiet, still state of consciousness. The therapy was started by a guy named, Harold Dull (sans irony) in 1980 at Harbin Hot Springs in California, and it has Zen Buddhism underpinnings.

One encounters refreshingly unconventional practices while living on a remote island. I had booked the session as part of a weeklong spiritual retreat in the midst of a secluded rainforest. Completely ignorant of what lay ahead, I strolled up to the appointment as if it were some sort of a resort day spa, and could not have anticipated how "woodsy" the setting was until I arrived. There was a small clearing where a large above-ground pool awaited near a small pool-house. The weather that afternoon was typical of the island of Maui—room temperature and a light breeze.

The French female practitioner, who was to be my Watsu guide, casually appeared wearing a black fishnet bathing suit that I was certain my mother had worn in the sixties. I couldn't have made this up; it was actually happening. There was a lot of data coming at me as she led me to the doughboy pool for my rebirthing. I couldn't help but notice how much she looked and sounded like Claudine Longet (a famous French chanteuse from the 1960s who could, kind of, sing).

Adding to the jitters I was experiencing was the small detail that during a Watsu session, the participant typically wears no clothing—no black fishnet for me. Let me make it absolutely clear that there was nothing remotely sexual about this predicament (unless the birds, watching from the trees above, had some interesting take on the situation). Awkward would be a better description of my feelings, though Claudine was completely nonplussed by either the situation or my nudity.

In a matter of moments, I found myself chest high in salt water, staring anxiously into Claudine's eyes as I awaited further instruction.

Silence.

More silence.

Suddenly I felt hyperaware of everything as the world seemed to freeze, I heard birds in the distance and took notice of the sun highlighting the freshly bleached mustache on the French lady's upper lip. Uncomfortable with the quiet, I finally murmured, "Um, I'm not exactly sure what to do." Claudine purred softly, "Zee Watzu eez not about doing ... it eez about **not doing**."

With that, I ceased all support from my legs, allowing me to plunge into the water. With a confidently swift move, she tied me like a pretzel, somehow curling me into a fetal position resting on top of the water. As she slowly swung me around the pool in back-and-forth rotations, utilizing one of those floating cylinders usually used by small children. She never let me get below chin-deep, amazing! I remember thinking, *How did she not get any water up my nose?* Within moments I forgot about my nerves, my nakedness, and her mustache as I drifted into a unique meditative state of "letting go" that I would recommend to anyone. (With or without a French lady, though I believe the accent was part of the hypnotics of it all.)

Among the insights provided by my time in the Watsu pool was the realization of just how hard it is to do nothing—to ride along, rather than drive for change. Being a service superhero is a lot like surfing, in that the practice requires a constant balance of physically making/letting things happen simultaneously.

> "To Listen First means not only to really *listen*
> (to genuinely seek to understand another person's thoughts, feelings,
> experience, and point of view), but to do it *first* (before you try to
> diagnose, influence or prescribe)."
> —Stephen M.R. Covey, *The Speed of Trust*

BE QUIET SO CUSTOMERS CAN ANSWER THEIR OWN QUESTIONS!

Never ever try to win an argument with a disgruntled customer, no matter how wrong they are or how right you are; it's a useless exercise that a service professional knows to avoid. This is when listening can become a weapon/tool for solving conflict because you have to stop introducing data long enough for the customer is to hear themselves talk. In fact, when a customer is on a tirade (justified or not), implore them to talk more! Only, make sure you're making genuine eye contact when you do.

First, more than anything, people want to feel heard and understood when detailing a grievance. Second, the more you allow a guest or client hear themselves vent, the more likely they are to realize they're more upset than they probably need to be. I have had the experience of hearing myself register a self-righteous complaint only to realize I've overreacted. In many cases, once customers have communicated a complaint, they prefer to drop the whole thing, or at least become easier to mollify.

The act of trying to win an argument with a customer is, in effect, attempting to convince someone they're wrong. I don't know about you, but being made to feel wrong rarely soothes my dissatisfaction with a service foul. Have you ever been guilty of this? Be quiet and listen to your customers so they can do most of the work obtaining a solution. Sometimes we really do have to just stop talking to gain power over a situation.

Note to call-center employees: I want to emphasize the special challenges facing employees of call centers who depend on their ability to move a transaction along as quickly as possible, or get to the core of an emergency event expediently. For you, the art of saying the right thing might not be nearly as important as asking the right thing. As opposed to interrupting the caller in order to redirect the conversation, focus on your foundational questioning to drive interactions. Are you asking the right questions? A caller will judge your credibility immediately based on the first questions asked.

BE QUIET SO YOU CAN ANSWER YOUR OWN QUESTIONS

Another wonderful reason for being quiet is the opportunity to hear yourself think. As long as we keep talking about what's already happened or what may go wrong in the future, we can't listen to "now." Being present—remember? The solution is floating around in someone's mind somewhere already; right now, someone has the information you want to hear—listen for it.

Quieting the mind is more difficult for some of us, especially for those who find traditional meditation to be excruciating. Some find stillness and quiet by actually making sounds. People practicing transcendental meditation find their own personal tone or mantra to repeat, while others find powerful tranquility by chanting, "Namyo-ho-renge-kyo." No judgment here, only encouragement. Inner peace is a very personal thing but whatever method you choose will require **steady, consistent practice**.

You may have noticed a pattern within the first five skills of the service superhero: they all require mastering the art of stopping. Holding off on action until intention is identified, embracing our ignorance to make way for knowledge, releasing the constraints of our personal vision to see things through another's eyes, being still enough to be present, or clamming up long enough to truly listen—these skills all demand the discipline of *not doing* in balance with *doing*.

"Listening is a magnetic and strange thing, a creative force. The friends who listen to us are the ones we move toward. When we are listened to, it creates us, makes us unfold and expand."
—Karl A. Menniger, author and founder of the
Menniger Psychiatric Foundation

CHAPTER TWELVE:
THE TEN SKILLS OF THE SERVICE SUPERHERO
#6. SERVING WITH SAFETY

"One earnest worker can do more by personal suggestion to prevent accidents than a carload of safety signs."
—E.R. Brown, *Making Paper*

DON'T STAY CALM!

Now that we've established the first foundational skills of INTENTION, KNOWLEDGE, PRESENCE, VISION, and LISTENING you may be feeling anxious and ready to put your superpowers to work in order to create magical wow-moments for your customers.

Slow down there, cowboy! Before we can dazzle anyone with service, we have to make certain they're safe and alive first.

Disney does some amazing pyrotechnic displays every night. They'd be even more spectacular if safety weren't an issue and no one minded fireworks shimmering down on their newly purchased mouse ears. After all, you've got to live through something in order to want to recommend the experience to somebody else.

In my earliest days of training, I was tasked with imploring new-hires to "stay calm" when encountering an emergency situation. I gave this up after about a year, having realized it's a complete waste of time. Not only do very few people have the natural ability of achieving serenity during crisis, I've come to believe customers would prefer focus over calm. Someone in trouble might not be able to detect how calm you are, but they will be able to judge your focus.

Earlier we established that there's no business BUT show business because everything involves a performance technique, even safety. That scene we encounter as we negotiate our way through airport security is, largely, for show. The same is true as one enters a theme park; the most security is being provided by cast members who are not costumed for security. Take a look around the next time you go to a theme park and see if there is a mature-yet-robust "tourist" lounging on a bench.

When coaching new employees on the importance of "performing security," I would share one of those Disney legends I alluded to earlier. The stories have certainly been embellished over time for both purpose and romance, but they prove a point in a memorable way. Here is one such story.

"KNOCK IT OFF—IT'S NOT THAT BAD!"

This legend begins with a typical beginning of a typical day at a Disney theme park: The rope is dropped and guests flood in like mice with a mission. The smartest thing a cast member can do is get out of the way. It's best to stake a spot on the curb and feverishly wave them on as they dash towards their first destination. It's a sea of humanity headed in one direction, usually, only one particular day, a couple of cast members noticed a single guest with a different objective—she wanted to cross the street. This is like trying to traverse a raging river.

There were more than a couple of eye-catching things about this solo guest. First, the woman was quite elderly but highly polished for her day at the park, looking as if she was ready for New Year's Eve. She had an enormously large hairdo festooned with little white flowers, and her arms were adorned with what appeared to be several pounds of Turquoise jewelry. All the clothing she had chosen involved a lot of "sparkle," but most noticeable were the lady's shoes, which would have been deemed dangerous due to their height by most reasonable people. The cast members on the curb might not have noticed the woman or her efforts to cross the street had she not been decorated, as they described later, like a tiny parade float.

Tentatively, she looked both ways before delicately stepping off the curb to cross the busy thoroughfare. For a split second, the cast members were shocked but transfixed by the act they were witnessing, like watching a really old lady trying to cross a freeway on stilts. Slowly, very slowly, she negotiated her way across the street, but this is where the shoes were her downfall, literally. One of the heels caught the cement curb, and she began to tip slowly and fall like a wee Christmas tree chopped down by a child.

Before I go any further, I'll tell you THE WOMAN WAS NOT HURT, thankfully. But she didn't know this yet and, like a small kid, could not decide if she was hurt or embarrassed—children do this all the time when they fall down in public and, apparently, we don't grow out of it.

It could barely be heard at first, but after a second, she began what was a mixture of groaning and whining. Even though the cast members leapt into action almost immediately with the intention of "staying calm," there was just one little problem: The woman had no intention or desire to be calm, and she didn't want anyone else indulging in it either. Making the situation worse was the fact that a growing crowd had ceased heading towards their first attraction to attend the "show" that was unfolding before their eyes. This seemed to trigger louder wailing, which only served to draw a bigger crowd. Pretty soon there were over 300 people watching a little old lady dressed like a party girl hollering, "I may have hurt myself—waaaaaaaaaaah!"

This is where the scene took an unfortunate turn, as one of the cast members panicked and hollered, "EVERYBODY JUST CALM DOWN!" at the top of his lungs. Then came the capper, the icing on a horrible cake, as he went on, "Let's all KNOCK IT OFF—it's not that bad!" It was like one of those scenes in a movie where a detective slaps a hysterical witness so they'll "snap out of it." This lady snapped all right.

In a twinkling of an eye, it was as if the park had been sucked into a vacuum. The world fell still and silent as everyone digested the fact that they'd just seen a Disney employee totally lose it on stage. The fallen guest, especially, looked as though she'd witnessed an assault—her own.

Now, Disney legends are stories passed down generationally through interpretation, but I can tell you this one actually happened exactly like this because I was there … and it was me! I was the idiot who lost my mind for a second and did not stay or act calm to say the least. I'd forgotten my own credo about all business being show business. Thankfully, I was forgiven by everyone, probably due to my obvious, unequivocal contrition—I said I was sorry several hundred times and clearly meant it.

On most occasions it has been my habit to be gracious, and no one would refer to me as cruel (I reiterate, the lady in the story was not really injured, just embarrassed), and yet I managed to come off like a real thoughtless ass because I forgot that there's a big difference between staying calm and acting calm. Just like there's a big difference between enjoying the company of every customer you encounter, and acting like you enjoy the company of every customer you encounter. You may say, "But I don't want to act—that would be disingenuous." No, it's a performance technique, and it goes on in every business. Trust me, I have it on good authority that the sight of our physical ailments occasionally disgust the doctors we see, yet they never show us. Well, hopefully not.

As you may imagine, most of the serious injuries taking place at theme parks are not happening in front of guests at all. A preponderance of the accidents that take place involve employees, and most are a result of either rushing or carelessness. These are probably the leading contributors to accidents in your current workplace as well. The other might be lack of knowledge.

The safety protocol at your place of work may vary, but the five most important pieces of information to arm yourself with are:

- Know your exit routes in case of fire, natural disaster, or (I'm sad to say) an active shooter.
- If you operate machinery, pay close attention to wear and maintenance—know the limits of the machine's capacity to function.
- Make yourself aware of any chemical substances you come into contact with, both their purpose and dangers.
- Wash your hands more often than you think you should.
- It's better to be late to work than dead.

Louie Gravance

"Tomorrow: your reward for working safely today."
—Attributed to Robert Pelton, author of *Come Back Alive*

CHAPTER THIRTEEN:
THE TEN SKILLS OF THE SERVICE SUPERHERO
#7. SERVING WITH COURTESY

"A brave heart and a courteous tongue.
They shall carry thee far through the jungle, manling."
—Rudyard Kipling, *The Jungle Book*

All right, you service superheroes, you've been patient, you've focused your energy and studied consistently. You've established what you want to be, and how and why you're going to be it—not necessarily in that order. You're anxious and eager to create magical service moments customers will be talking about for years, so let's get started. As graduating wizards in the Harry Potter books are eventually told, "You may now use your wands!"

Armed with intention and knowledge, many of you are already exceeding expectations and creating wow-experiences for customers in your worlds. Though not always the most powerful skill, COURTESY is the most visible of the service super-strengths. Think of a play you may have seen where the writing, direction, and sets were wonderful but the acting was amateurish. Consider demonstrations of courtesy as the "acting" in your show.

During one of my seminars, we do an exercise called "Good Show/Bad Show" when we focus on understanding and exceeding customer expectations. The most common behavior demonstrated when I ask participants to show me what Good Show looks like in their business is giving something away for free to the customer. "This is on the house," they'll say, or "Come back for free next time." Giving away something for free is not the way to add value to your customer relationships. In fact, freebies can devalue your service.

Sometimes it's better to aim the power of courtesy at the heart, rather than the head. What does that mean? Showing is better than telling. Attempting to impress customers with information about your product or service is aiming for the head, i.e., the intellect. But every transaction is an emotional transaction, so aiming for the heart will always have a greater impact, even if nobody gets anything for free.

Person to person, good service doesn't cost any more than bad service—courtesy is free. Invariably, the most substantial service experiences you'll ever create will cost no one anything at all in terms of dollars.

THE ELF WHO MADE GROWN-UPS CRY

The state of Florida does not kid around about Christmas. The Sunshine State approaches the holiday season with a gusto one might not expect from such a tropical locale. Other warm climates where I have lived (Hollywood, Hawaii, Palm Desert) have all treated the Christmas season with a touch of irony and humor, not Florida. Florida stubbornly insists on a snowy, winter wonderland regardless of weather. This dedication to Yuletide spectacle is even more in evidence at the theme parks where, from October to January, the entire resort is wrapped like a gift box with flashing lights.

Since we've already established the fact of my diminutive physicality, it shouldn't be any surprise that I've "done time" as an elf more than once. One of those times happened to be my very first Christmas as a WDW cast member. I was already thirty-two years old and had thought my days in green tights were over, but there I stood in the center of the park holding the crowd until Santa Goofy and his magical reindeer arrived. In addition to my green legs, I had a whimsical tunic, pointy ears, and bells on my cap and shoes. (The horrified look on my father's face upon seeing me as an elf is something forever seared into my brain.) Making the scene even more surreal was faux snow gently falling from the rooftops while Bing Crosby sang "White Christmas" on a constant loop.

Still, I attacked the assignment with the same pixie-dusted enthusiasm I infused into most tasks and went about spreading good cheer as one of Santa Goofy's helpers. This would require being in close contact with a massive crowd, waiting while Mr. Crosby crooned continuously in the background.[11]

One evening, just a few days before Christmas, a small family of three caught my attention—a woman with two boys in their late teens. (I would later learn that the middle-aged mother was originally from Cuba and this was her first time at a Disney

---

11 Now is a good time to address the stress involved working in "song locations." People can get tired of the song "It's a Small World" waiting in line for fifteen minutes, so imagine forty hours a week! People ask, "Do you just tune it out?" The answer is yes, and no. The monotony eases over time, but the problem is the syncopation of the sounds backstage. The hydraulic pistons operating the animatronics make a rhythmic hiss that becomes part of the constant melody you hear, even on the ride home. This is one of the reasons that people who operate the "song rides" are rotated to other rides on a regular basis.

park.) What caught my attention was the special affection shared amongst the three of them. The love these two boys had for their mom was evident. The kids provided giggles, hugs, and one was even giving the mother gentle "noogies" on the head. Now, I grew up with a loving family, but we were not generally physically affectionate—I never tried giving my mother noogies, not even in private. Perhaps this is one of the reasons I noticed these folks in the first place.

For some unknown reason, I felt compelled to look earnestly into this woman's eyes and softly say, "Wow, you must be a great mom. Your boys clearly love you very much. You know, a lot of guys their age wouldn't feel so cool about showing off how much they love their mom—your kids are crazy about you." Even though English was her second language, she seemed to understand every word as she looked at me, paused, and began to cry. *Oh no!*, I thought, *this is not my intention at all.* I'm not exactly sure what my intention was at the time, but it was definitely not making someone cry. It's terrible making a child cry while dressed like an elf—it's even worse bringing an adult to tears.

Feeling clumsy and not knowing what to do, I backed up as if I'd accidentally lit a Christmas tree on fire. The silly bells on my boots and hat were all I could hear as I slowly retreated, making the scene even more surreal. I become uncomfortable when strangers cry in front of me, and it's one of the few times I'm lost for words. Not knowing what to do I lamely offered, "Well, have a magical holiday," in a squeaky elf voice and disappeared. Really? Fifteen years in show business and that was the best I could come up with? What had I done? Was she even their mother? Had I made some childless nanny weep?

Covering my backside, I immediately went to the stage

manager and blurted, "I just made a lady cry, and I totally didn't mean to!"

"What did you do to her?" she asked.

"I told her she was a good mom."

The next day, dressed as me, while Bing and Santa Goofy were doing their thing, I saw the same, small Cuban woman rushing towards me from down the street yelling, "Uno photo, uno photo, uno PHOTO!" The same lady I'd managed to make cry the day before suddenly wanted my picture taken with her, and I wasn't exactly sure why. Neither was I sure posing with her was such a good idea, as I was afraid of causing tears again. One of the boys took the photo, she hugged me, began to tear-up again, whispered, "Feliz Navidad," then vanished into the crowd. I still had no idea what had transpired but at least I was pretty sure the crying I witnesses had been "nice tears" somehow.

Having forgotten about the encounter, I was quite surprised when, three months later, the same woman could be heard joyously shrieking, "Uno photo, uno photo," as she rushed towards me through an audience—different show, different park. I was not wearing green tights or pointy ears, but she knew it was me. Again, she hugged me, got misty-eyed and disappeared after having our picture taken.

This happened again at least three more times over the next two years! It was never the same show, sometimes not even the same park, but she'd find me and repeat the ritual, and I grew happy to see her. Over time, she insisted I refer to her as "Mamacita," and I obliged. There must have been many, many rolls of film of just the two of us.

One day, a supervisor handed me a manila envelope, the kind we would get that usually contained a guest letter or compliment forwarded through guest services, with a copy sent to our personnel file. I pulled out the document and saw the words "FROM THE DESK OF MICHAEL EISNER," our larger-than-life CEO at the time. Mamacita had managed to get a letter to Mr. Eisner detailing her first time meeting me, which also happened to be her first time in a Disney park. The letter would go on to explain that she had pre-paid nine months early for that first visit, which was to include her two sons, herself and her "Pappi," meaning her father. Sadly, he had passed away one month prior to the trip, leaving Mamacita not sure she was up to the vacation planned for so long. Her boys, thinking the trip might be just the thing to pull them all out of the funk they'd been experiencing, convinced her to go anyway.

As it turned out the boys were right, in a way. While the getaway, indeed, pulled the kids out of their funk, it had only served to make their mom even sadder. I had no idea I had encountered her at her breaking point the first time I laid eyes on her. It seems that the sound of Bing Crosby singing "White Christmas," which I had grown tired of, was the emotional trigger for this nice lady to bottom out emotionally. The playful rough-housing I had witnessed was the boys trying to convince her not to take the bus home to Miami the next day—they wanted her to stay. This was the scene I had ignorantly strolled into and the exact moment I popped up with, "You must be a great mom!" Mamacita finished the letter with, "Mr. Eisner I had no idea that there would be a little angel there to remind me of all I had to be thankful of. I will never forget him."

Okay, first, I'm aware that that is embarrassingly sweet and kind of hard to take, but the point is this: I'd worked a whole lot harder than that to get a guest compliment before. In fact, I could be shameless in my efforts to elicit positive feedback from guests, and facilitated innumerable magical wow-moments. Still, it's remarkable that of all my achievements during a span of three decades at Disney, one of the things that I will most be remembered for is a simple act of courtesy—a time I simply looked into another person's face, remained present, and said, "You must be a great mom." That's it, period. No fireworks. Mickey Mouse didn't show up out of nowhere. Nobody got anything for free. One single, genuine, caring remark was all it took to create one of the greatest acts of magic I ever got to deliver. That's what I mean by aiming for the heart and not the head with utilizing service superpowers.

NON-NEGOTIABLES

Just as there are basic fundamental moves every great dancer must have, and classic throws all great pitchers must master, there are certain must-haves in the world of service. The very least a service superhero can do is as follows:

The single most important service action is to ALWAYS look happy to see the customer!

Make consistent eye contact with every customer.

No eating, drinking, or smoking in front of your audience.

Never lean on anything or sit while customers are standing.

Always gesture with an open palm rather than pointing.

Never cut a customer off mid-sentence.

The words "I don't know" are forbidden unless followed with "but let's find out!"

Do not treat a customer as though they cannot afford the product your selling, even when you think they can't.

Use the words "please" and "thank you" as often as possible.

The fastest way to drive someone out of your store is to say, "May I help you?"

Remember that every client or patient is an opportunity, and every cause made for courtesy has a definite, if immeasurable, effect. Great service serves the server first—whether we can see it immediately or not. In this way service is, in fact, transactional.

"Courtesies of a small and trivial character are the ones which strike the deepest in the grateful and appreciating heart."
—Henry Clay

CHAPTER FOURTEEN:
THE TEN SKILLS OF THE SERVICE SUPERHERO
#8. SERVING WITH SHOWMANSHIP

"Like the theater, offering food and hospitality to people is a matter of showmanship, and no matter how simple the performance, unless you do it well, with love and originality, you have a flop on your hands."
—James Beard

O ne of the most unexpectedly scary things you may ever see is Mickey Mouse walking towards you backstage because it's probable that the only time you've seen Mickey, he's either in a still photograph or on screen. It's easy to underestimate the performance technique required to bring those costumed characters to life. These entertainers can't waste their energy outside the guest's view so, as they walk to and from set, Mickey often walks like an exhausted young adult concerned about overheating. Without the physical showmanship we're used to seeing, Mickey looks like a dead doll moving maniacally towards you. In that moment, it looks exactly like what it is: a large rubber head. People bring it to life.

For those who find the parks "plastic" or "fake," this is all they see. To some, a theme park is nothing more than a shopping mall with rides and, literally speaking, this is true. It takes the emotional investment of both guest and cast member to create magic for the enterprise.

During first-day orientation, I would tell new cast members that there was a choice we had to make every day: Magical memories, or robots and rubber heads. Because the fact of the matter is that both points of view can be true simultaneously.

"The secret of showmanship consists not of what you really do, but what the mystery-loving public thinks you do."
—Harry Houdini

SELLING MAGIC WANDS FOR A LIVING

Arguably there is no better example of how showmanship helps to create a perfect, magical service moment than the Ollivander's Wand Shop experience at the Universal theme park's The Wizarding World of Harry Potter™ in Hollywood and Orlando. Here, several lines of business seamlessly come together to pull off one of the greatest theatrical-retail experiences ever created. One doesn't have to be steeped in Potter lore to appreciate the commitment to detail or have one's breath taken away by the sheer artistry exhibited. For the hardcore Potter fan, however, this can often be a nearly religious experience. I have personally witnessed many a millennial sob with a mix of joy and childhood nostalgia at their first sight of Hogwarts School.

It was my experience and good fortune to be a part of the opening of Diagon Alley and the launch of the wand shop "experience"—a splendid mash-up of retail, entertainment, park operations, and storytelling. While strictly limited as to what I can/should divulge, allow me to break down the experience from the guest POV to support my points and this book's purpose.

For those not expert in the world and ways of Harry Potter

(I was not at the beginning of my involvement), this is all you really need to know: three kids have magical powers in wizardry, they go to a secret school for wizards where they encounter and, seven books later, defeat evil. That's pretty much it … not to take away from the literary success. Suffice it to say that the seven- to nine-minute show/experience with the "wandkeeper" replicates an important scene in both the initial book and first film PRECISELY where the children are "paired" with their magic wand. And by this, I mean line-by-line, word-for-word, with little to no deviation. This is necessary partly because so much of the audience is intimately familiar with the source material and patrons can be seen mouthing the dialogue as the wandkeeper facilitates the scene. This is also a testament to the awesome creative control of the books' author, J.K. Rowling.[12]

It is with this kind of attention to detail that makes the shops appear exactly as they're illustrated in the movies: small, cramped, and quaint. Some would say ridiculously small for the "out-put" (theme-park jargon indicating how many guests an hour can enjoy the experience), typically considered necessary for a busy attraction. As no more than thirty guests enter the tiny, crowded shop, they encounter the sights and smells of a room filled to the brim with thousands of "dusty" wands. Familiar strains of the film's music may be heard in the hall and, to many, it feels like they just walked into the movie.

"The wand chooses the wizard," the wandkeeper intones as the doors are shut and the scene begins. He or she then finds

---

12 It is rumored that the reason Ms. Rowling's work was brought to life at Universal's parks rather than Disney's was due to this kind of control. Disney was reportedly doing the we-know-best game, while Universal took the you-know-best path with the author. I wasn't there, but I'd wager a lot of money on the validity of this scenario, if I were a betting man.

the perfect participant among the crowd to mimic the pivotal moment where Harry's wand chooses him. "You are here for your wand," is exclaimed as the participant is brought forward into the show. The "chosen one" is ideally around ten or eleven years old (the same age as Harry in the book), but it can be literally anyone in the room the wand wizard deems suitable.

Of course, the wandkeepers are highly skilled actors, many with decades of experience in more than one discipline of performing. Each actor must be able to pull off an English or Scottish accent (reapproved every year) and must adhere to the script's text almost slavishly. This is one of the only park performing jobs where improvisation is nearly forbidden and monitored closely.

"Perhaps a wand of ivy," the character posits before requesting the participant perform any number of acts of magic using the potential wand, for example: "Brighten up the room with the tip of this wand!" But, just as in the source material, things go terribly amiss for the aspiring wizard, and it's made clear that "this is definitely not your wand!" A second wand is tried only to find that it, too, is not the right fit.

Suddenly yet subtly, the movie music which underscores this segment of the film can be heard. The wandkeeper, after several minutes of getting an impression of the guest and which wand might make a good pairing, mutters, "The wand chooses the wizard," before slowly attempting a connection with a third wand. Will this be the wand that selects you or your child?

Sure enough, the instant the hopeful touches the "correct" wand, just like in the movie, the room explodes with light, wind, and a heavenly orchestra heralding the perfect match. All kidding aside, this is often a very emotional moment, and tears are not atypical as the character whispers, "This wand has chosen you," as the scene is closed out and the guest is handed off to a "wand assistant."

It is at this moment that one of the smoothest pass-offs in the history of retail takes place. The family is politely ushered into the hallway, where the skilled merchandise attendant exclaims, "Congratulations on being chosen!" Then, with all the earnestness of a hungry puppy, they look into the eyes of the parents and ask, "Will you be purchasing *your* wand today?" Bam! How many customers do you think shrug and say, "Nah, I don't think so"? The answer is, not very many.

Think of all the perfect points of synergy that must come together to create this unforgettable guest experience and piece of theatrical-retail in order to sell what is essentially a stick. That's right, a stick, and at the time of this writing, a $52 stick. Or is it? It is whatever it looks, sounds, smells, and feels like to the customer.

It takes a lot of people's efforts to transform that stick into a wand. There is, of course, the writer who imagined the scenario in the first place. Also, sketch artists, engineers, construction workers, manufacturers, truck drivers, merchandise employees, custodial workers, special effects professionals, musicians, and actors—all have to work in concert to make that stick magical.

Figuratively, this same choice is being acted out all around us, including where you work too. It's a constant decision we make every day: what's it going to be today, sticks or wands?

NEVER LET 'EM SEE YOU SWEAT!

There used to be a deodorant commercial with the slogan, "Never let 'em see you sweat." There is a huge divide in opinion among show business professionals on that kind of attitude. Some believe one's performance technique should appear smooth and effortless (think Harry Connick Jr.). Others believe an audience likes to see how hard you're working (think Liza Minnelli). Myself, I've always been one to "play to the cheap seats" as they say—never known for subtlety. However, in your setting, smooth and effortless may be more appropriate and more akin to your authentic self. It's a choice all service superheroes make, and sometimes different occasions call for different approaches. Different swords for different battles.

When working for tips, I always found it useful to let them see how hard I was working, without being too distracting or dramatic. The same is true as a public speaker. You may be surprised how many professional speakers turn on their PowerPoint presentations and follow along. The energy I try to show during my speaking "concerts" is a way of showing the audience that I'm engaged and committed to the time we're sharing. And it's a good thing to show people what your intention is.

The necessary performance technique of a tax accountant or surgeon is, of course, entirely different. These are professional services best served as if to say, "You're in good, steady hands, and this won't be difficult because I know what I'm doing." Either way, both are performance styles that show your clients that you're committed to their satisfaction.

How will I know I'm safe doing business with you if you don't show me? How will I know you're an expert in finance if you don't show me? How will I know how good your product is if you don't show me? How will I know I can trust you if you don't show me? How will I know you understand my needs if you don't show me?

It isn't good enough for you to tell me of your worth—you have to show me. Since cave drawings, communication has been a matter of storytelling and conveying ideas. We're "showing" all of the time; our personal degree and style of showmanship dictates much of our ability to communicate. Just looking happy to see me, whether you are or aren't, employs showmanship. Giving your customers good, clear directions is a matter of knowledge and showmanship. The sound made as a plate is set on a table is showmanship, as is opening a champagne bottle for dinner guests. Even doctors "perform" surgery.

Exceeding expectations when you just don't feel like it definitely demands showmanship. Staying consistent with your personal showmanship will require the ability to see your performance through the eyes of your service recipients. This requires the skill of memory, but let's not get ahead of ourselves.

"We become just by performing just action, temperate by performing temperate actions, brave by performing brave action."
—Aristotle

CHAPTER FIFTEEN:
THE TEN SKILLS OF THE SERVICE SUPERHERO
#9. SERVING WITH EFFICIENCY

*"Conscienceless efficiency is no match for
efficiency quickened by conscience."*
—Kelly Miller

BEING EFFICIENT

It might surprise/please you to know that our examination of efficiency as a service superpower will be efficiently brief. Why? Because we're usually talking about systems and processes when discussing efficiency in the workplace, and I never pretend to be an expert on a client's specific line of business. Even though I've designed and developed training for large banks, I have never tried to pass myself off as a wizard in finance—because I'm not. Neither am I an expert on operating a senior living facility, being a claims adjuster, running a restaurant, owning a funeral home, or any other of the hundreds of businesses I've worked with or spoken to. This is something I make perfectly clear at the outset: I don't want to communicated under false pretenses.

Rather, my expertise is putting your expertise in a workable context for delivering excellent service. I will not pretend to know your specific processes, but I can help you keep them in perspective. In the Disney module of Safety, Courtesy, Show, and Efficiency, you'll notice that process comes last in the equation. That's because a break in your processes/systems is the most likely of the four values to be forgiven.

Earlier I mentioned that I focus on context more than content when creating training programs, and the same will be true of this chapter. I would like to discuss how two previously explored superpowers—knowledge and showmanship—frame the context with which you use efficiency to wow customers.

PERFORMING EFFICIENCY WITH KNOWLEDGE

You would be shocked to know how much your employer is spending to stay in business, even if they're spending too little on your service expertise. This is something I chastise small business owners about all the time. I tell them that unless you're cheating your employees, share the numbers with them. It is so easy to disconnect from the cost of something you're not paying for, but if you know the financial metrics of the place where you work, you have a different appreciation of its value. How much is the rent? How much to have IT support bring the registers back online? How much is spent on advertising?

Recently, at a local market, a young lady bagged my groceries. Her method was one you've probably seen: one item to a bag. Instead of professionally bagging the twenty items in three bags, she found it easier to accomplish with twelve. The manager witnessed this and said, nicely but frustrated, to the young woman, "What are you doing? This is a way you can help me, you can put more than one thing in a bag." It never dawned on the employee that every one of those bags costs money, and it would take virtually no time at all to waste a thousand of them.

Even if, like many Americans, you're underpaid for the value you bring, you should understand the many ancillary costs that come with you as an employee, such as social security contributions, uniforms, insurance (even if it's just to insure you while you're there).

PERFORMING EFFICIENCY WITH SHOWMANSHIP

My favorite example of a frontline cast member creating a simple system for efficiency-utilizing-showmanship took place at Disneyland in 1960, and it's still being used today.

As you can imagine (or experienced personally) the family can be pretty amped-up as you arrive at the parking lot of a massive tourist attraction. You're trying to follow signals to your appointed spot, the kids are spinning in the backseat, your husband is asking about tickets, or maybe the sight of the Matterhorn is stealing focus. Regardless of the specifics, the odds of forgetting where you parked are astronomical. Making things worse is the fact that this is quite possibly a rental car, and you're not going to be good at identifying it or describing it. "We're in a white rental!" can be heard every night from a panicked guest. Time for a piece of "efficiency magic," as a double-size golf cart rolls up and a frequent scene is played out. The cast member reassures the guest/family that the car will be found even if it takes some time. Worried family climbs aboard the cart and the hunt begins. Casually, the cast member will ask a series of questions, as conversationally as possible: Did you have fun? Was it a full day? Was it a long day? What was the first thing you did? Did you have breakfast first or did you head for the rides? Sounds fun, what time did you get here? What the cast member is doing sneakily is trying to decipher what time the family arrived in the parking lot.

A college kid came up with a crude diagram (below), splitting up the parking lot into sections where arrival times could be logged in increments of fifteen minutes. This way, seemingly like magic, the cast member could significantly narrow down the possible locations of the lost car and bring the guests' panic to an abrupt end. It would be a great way to save the finale of the day's adventure.

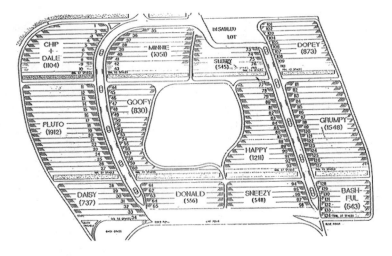

The concept is so simple that it's practically childish, but it is evidence of how a marriage of system and showmanship can create emotional outcomes in service. Efficiency and emotion are not mutually exclusive.

Learn to read your audience. Remember, not every customer wants to become friends, and not everyone is looking for a "memorable" service interaction (a lot of folks like their pixie dust in very low doses). But there are instances when the best service is where nothing extraordinary happens at all and takes place in a split second.

EFFICIENT BALANCE

Just as our left brain is always attempting to work in balance with our right, there is a struggle within every organization for control. The fight is about whether our systems are serving us, or we're serving our systems. In an effort to be as efficient as possible, companies will create processes and systems with very good intentions, but if you work for one organization for a significant amount of time, you will experience times of imbalance when you find yourself (at least periodically) slavishly serving a system that controls to a greater degree than it serves.

The overwhelming message to the service superhero is to use processes and systems to deliver the power of efficiency; don't allow them to use you. Don't allow your systems to use your customers, either, and you'll be fine—easier said than done, I know, so this is why the last super-skill is so vital.

> "I'll take 50 percent efficiency to get 100 percent loyalty."
> —Samuel Goldwyn

CHAPTER SIXTEEN
THE TEN SKILLS OF THE SERVICE SUPERHERO
#10. SERVING WITH YOUR MEMORY

"Your memory is the glue that binds your life together; everything you are today is because of your amazing memory. You are a data collecting being, and your memory is where your life is lived."
—*Kevin Horsley, UNLIMITED MEMORY*

Memory is a service power we all have but rarely use; in fact, we're sloppy and careless with it. That is a shame because it's the best "reset tool" we have. For those of us inundated with tasks, having a reset button that reconnects us with our fundamental intentions is essential for focus. "Forgetting" is the single greatest nemesis to the service superhero, our Kryptonite.

To fight against this, I strongly suggest establishing a service "reconnection memory." The average person inclined to read this far into the book is prewired to provide service, and exceeded many a customer's expectations already, so you have many memories to draw from. Do you remember any of instances of service excellence in your life? When was the last time you truly dwelled on what you've already done and been? Because of the service moments you have provided, at this very second, someone might be:

- Boarding a plane for an exciting adventure.
- Alive because of tires you sold them.
- Holding their child because you recognized a warning sign.
- Confident going into an important job interview because of the outfit you suggested and sold to them.
- Having a romantic memory because of table service you created.
- Still in their home because of insurance you provided.
- Advancing to higher education because of something you taught them.
- Getting a part in an important show because of the support you gave them.
- Finding the help they need due to your counsel on a suicide prevention call.

The emotional outcomes of your efforts are innumerable, yet they are easily forgotten in the midst of our ever-mounting tasks. This is why the use of a reconnection memory is an invaluable discipline to develop and maintain. A reconnection memory brings you back into the customers' point of view, allowing you to see things anew through their eyes.

Release all of your current prejudices and look at "the movie" as if it were the first time. Maybe you can find a memory that reconnects you with what it's like to be your customer, client, or patient.

TRIGGERING MEMORY

We've established that all business is show business and that performers constantly use memory as a tool to conjure the right emotion for whatever scene they're playing or song they're singing. There are a multitude of powerful memory triggers available to us:

- Listening to music from various times in your life will transport your head to a previous time with little effort.
- Catching glimpses on YouTube of commercials you watched repeatedly as a child but haven't thought of in years.
- Looking at a yearbook or an old photo album—a great way to recognize how far you've come … or not.
- Revisit movies and shows you remember fondly. There has never been an easier time in history to do this.
- Reread books you weren't sophisticated enough to grasp the first time.
- Revisit fragrances from the past. For me, there is no more powerful memory trigger than the sense of smell. I know that whatever perfume my first-grade teacher wore is still in existence because I occasionally catch a whiff in a crowd and am immediately returned to 1964.

"We all have our time machines. Some take us back, they're called memories. Some take us forward, they're called dreams."

—Jeremy Irons

REMEMBERING WITH WALLY

It is only fair that I share with you my "reconnection memory."

In 1962, my grandparents owned a small restaurant that had the first color television I had ever laid eyes on. Every Sunday evening, the place would be closed and the family would gather to watch *Walt Disney's Wonderful World of Color*. My first memory of color TV includes a bright red tie around the neck of "Uncle Walt" himself.

My favorite part of the program wasn't the show itself but the segments Walt would do at the end promoting what was currently being "imagineered" for Disneyland. I never recall a moment in my life when I wasn't fascinated by that place. My favorite part of the show, however, was my father's *least* favorite because it meant the inevitable discussion about when we'd be making a trip to see what was coming next.

Dad had no interest in going to Disneyland, at all. He just didn't get it. Why would somebody want to drive four hours and spend a fortune to sit in a teacup? I'm sure that's how he saw it. "I can't get the time off right now," he'd say. "One of these days the boss will give me some time off and we'll make a trip down there." I was not a dim-witted child; by the time I was six, I was already aware he was giving me the brush-off. I knew he had weekends off.

My idea to overcome this obstacle was to approach the owner of the beer distribution company my father worked for and let him know he was being used as an excuse for not taking my brother and me to Disneyland. It was the annual Christmas party, thrown at his large home, where I earnestly informed him, "You know, I'm going to be eight this year and I STILL haven't gotten to Disneyland."

"*Really?*" he responded.

"Yes! And my dad says the reason we can't go is because *you* won't give him the time off." I accusingly wagged my finger at him. "So ... it would be really good if you could, you know, give him a break for Disneyland."

I can still recall the twinkle in the gentleman's eye as he

picked me up, hoisted me high into the air, and landed me on his knee. He then surveyed the crowd in search of my dad who had, just then, caught sight of me bouncing on the boss's knee. His face was already marked with dread as the man beckoned him over with one finger. "I hear your boy here hasn't been to Disneyland and it's my fault ... is that about it?" This guy had already had a couple of drinks and was enjoying this encounter immensely. Dad had no idea how to respond as the gentleman continued playfully: "I don't understand; we've all taken our kids to Disneyland." Gesturing around the room he continued, "Joe, Larry, Chuck, have all made the trip and had a helluva good time—I don't see why you can't take your kids, Tony. I mean, I give you weekends off, don't I? Next year, when we have this party, I wanna hear these kids have been to Disneyland."

We left the party shortly thereafter, and my father was quite unhappy ... but persuaded. It took until the next November, but he was determined to make it happen, even though our mother was very sick with the cancer she would eventually beat. We got up very early on November 15, 1966 and readied for what was the longest car ride of my life at the time. I remember the date because it was one month to the day before Walt Disney died, a day I'll never forget.

"Did you remember to get money?" my mother asked (a silly question, since my father never forgot how much something was going to cost).

"I took out a hundred dollars," he declared.

I was floored at what seemed to me like an enormous amount of cash, making the day feel even more significant.

We pulled into the parking lot at 12:30 in the afternoon. Though park historians would probably indicate this wasn't the prettiest era to see the park (Tomorrowland had just been bulldozed for an update), to me it was the gleaming wonderland I had imagined, maybe better. What surprised me the most was how much and how quickly Dad was taken in by it all.

He was particularly impressed with the cleanliness. It is impossible for anyone under the age of forty to comprehend how much the average American was exposed to cigarette smoking in the 1960s. People smoked in movie theaters, planes, elevators, restaurants, cars (with the windows rolled up), and, yes, amusement parks. (The term "theme park" hadn't been invented yet.) So, it's easy to forget something grown-ups used to marvel at and talk about: how fast your cigarette butts were swept from the ground after being dropped. This is one of the park's features my father was absolutely astounded by. "You won't believe it," he'd regale many times. "It's not fifteen seconds before somebody flies outta nowhere to sweep up the cigarette you just put out!" Pixie dust comes in many forms; regardless, he was on board.

At this point in Disneyland's history, one could still find the place nearly empty on a school day in November, and this was one of those days. This made it easy for my parents to navigate my younger brother and me around briskly from ride to ride. A lucky thing, since none of us had much experience with large crowds. Midway through the day, we strolled into a saloon where the "The Golden Horseshoe Revue" was enjoying the first season of a nearly four-decade run, still with its original cast. It was a classic musical comedy revue in a Western style. Coming from a very small town in an agricultural community, I had not yet been exposed to live theater in any form. Wow.

This was a tremendous amount of fresh data for me to process and I was transfixed. About two-thirds of the way through the performance, "the funny guy" showed up and proceeded to take over the show and make it his. His name was Wally Boag, and he was a remarkably gifted comedy performer who had a profound impact on many young people with showbiz aspirations.[13] Boag was smooth, fun, and unapologetically corny.

In the middle of his set, he would require the participation of one of the kids in the audience. I was in the right place at the right time, and Wally motioned for me to join him onstage. I wasn't prepared for any of this. There was no way I could have known how hot the spotlight was going to feel, or how it would blind you from seeing your parents in the audience. I stood petrified as this professional entertainer, who had already done the show several hundred times, attempted to keep things running smoothly. I had no response to his questions or cajoling and, to this day, I can remember being hypnotized by the dust particles floating in the light shining in my face as he tried to engage me.

This is the instant my life was permanently altered because he proceeded to use his service superpowers on me. Knowing exactly how to deal with a case like me, he took my hand, went down on one knee so we were head-to-head, and faced the audience with me. Three times, gently but firmly, he squeezed my hand and then swept his arm across the theater while whispering, "*Whooosh*" in my ear. And with that, he took responsibility for facilitating the moment we were sharing, and I finally took a breath. I looked into his face and then looked out at the audience. Once again, I looked into his face then out at the audience, and I felt strangely at home. At that second, I had no

---

13 Steve Martin was working at Disneyland at the time, and he writes glowingly in his autobiography of the influence Wally had on his comedy.

idea that, in twenty-five years, I would end up as "the funny guy" on a similar stage or that I would be performing the same bits in a show called the "Hoop-dee-doo Revue." I too eventually found myself with one lone child onstage going comatose exactly as I had done. What a marvelous gift to give back! With a huge bear rug on my head, I would go down on one knee, take their little hand in mine, give it three quick squeezes as my hand swept the audience and I say, "*Whooosh.*"

Suddenly, I was back to Neverland. I experienced everything through a child's eyes again: Everything looked the same, sounded the same, smelled the same, and it definitely *felt* the same. I would remember and reconnect with what I **intended** to be. This was my service reconnection memory, my reset, and I used it to bring me back into "now" and see things again through the guest's eyes.

I know you have a moment that will work just as well. If not, you'll make one, but try to *remember* all you've done already.

PROTECTING SUPER-SKILLS WITH MEMORY

Taking time to remember is like consistently working out physically—it builds and maintains strength. Remember the following:

- **Intention**, not just about what you're doing but what you're being.
- **Knowledge** of your company, your service, and your customers.
- **A Vision** of what things look like through your customers' eyes and feels like in their hearts.

- **Presence** in "now"—it's all we have.
- **Listening**—it'll give you the upper hand.
- **Safety** is always the most important thing.
- **Courtesy**—remember the strength of being nice.
- **Performance**—there's no business *but* show business.
- **Efficiency**—working smarter is always better than working faster. Systems should serve you in order to provide efficiency for your customers—not the other way around.

"I've learned that people will forget what you said, people will forget what you did, but people will never forget how you made them feel."
—*Maya Angelou*

CHAPTER SEVENTEEN:
THE TEN SKILLS OF THE SERVICE SUPERHERO
THE SECRET INGREDIENT

"Those grateful for glitter are gifted with diamonds."
—*Louie Gravance*

OH YES, AND SOMETHING I FORGOT...

In every version of *Peter Pan*, there is a sequence in which Peter teaches Wendy and her brothers to fly in order to get to Neverland. Peter instructs the Darling children that all they have to do is "think happy thoughts," and they'll be gifted with the ability to fly. Even though the children do their best to comply, they can't seem to get off the ground. After a brief frustration, Peter Pan realizes why happy thoughts alone aren't getting the job done: "Oh, there's something I forgot! DUST! Just a little bit of pixie dust." It seems that happy thoughts (even those fortified with faith and trust) needed one more magical ingredient for lift-off—one more ingredient necessary to bring power to all the other ingredients. For our purposes, metaphorically, that last magical ingredient of pixie dust is HUMILITY. This is as true for organizations as it is for individuals.

It has been my assignment to facilitate culture shifts in service for two of the largest financial institutions in the world. Both wanted to earn or regain customer loyalty by delivering premiere service experiences, and both had the goal of becoming a "most admired" company in their field. While both organizations saw improvements as a result of our service initiatives, only one of the two (Bank of America) was able to significantly change their culture enough to meet their goals. It took me a little while and a little more experience to understand why.

Bank of America approached the challenge with a true sense of humility. They knew they could do a better job serving clients and took responsibility for temporarily falling short. They embraced what they didn't know and opened themselves up to thinking differently. Leadership, of course, set the intention in motion, but even among the frontline associates, there was a collective focus on reinvention.

The second financial institution I worked with also wanted to improve customer satisfaction, but there was just the tiniest bit of arrogance living within a sizable faction. They didn't want to improve customer satisfaction as much as they wanted to raise customer satisfaction *scores*. Many within the organization thought the disconnect with their clients wasn't because they were delivering bad service. Rather, the customers just didn't "get it," because they "weren't sophisticated enough" to understand the products offered. The company wasn't interested in changing their service culture as much as they wanted to change the way customers felt about the service they were already getting. The second group had all the talent of the first but, collectively, lacked the necessary ingredient—humility. Without it, they couldn't really see themselves clearly.

The same is true for us personally. We've all worked with people who consistently deliver service with excellence yet never seem to capitalize on it. We've all been one of those people who, for a time, seems to be swimming wildly upstream. We become frustrated because, regardless of effort, we cannot seem to progress in our career. Subsequent self-judgment about our lack of progress only serves to define it, making things worse.

Be careful of frustrations. In no time at all, frustration evolves into resentment, and resentment is poison. Resentment might not negate the service moments enjoyed by your customers, but it will absolutely stall the benefits you perceive. Nothing dulls service superpowers quite like resentment.

I'm certainly not the only person who got too old to play kids on television after doing it until the age of twenty-five. Nor the only successful actor to end up waiting tables—I know lots of them. One thing most of them have in common is bitterness that's often profound and consuming. Like everything else in life, choice is a major component.

When I look back at some of the wonderful things I've been fortunate to achieve in my adult life, they were all possible due to a single choice. When I saw myself in my waiter uniform for the first time, I wasn't wise enough to understand the choice in front of me: arrogance or humility. Had I made the choice to resent where I had put myself, I would probably still be waiting tables and mad at the world. Quite a few folks make that choice. Instead, I invested 100 percent of myself in what was in front of me and found joy (and power) in service. By offering humility, I removed the obstacles in my way. Suddenly, it was like Mickey's white glove came out of the sky and placed me on another path, the one I'd been conjuring since childhood.

The thing is this, humility makes true gratitude possible, and gratitude provides grace. Nothing will magnify the effects of your service skills both for you and your customers like grace—nothing. Pay close attention to what is frustrating you while you can still be objective. You might be trying to send yourself a message about your need to change your environment before it changes you. Here are five signs of being "in the wrong place":

1. You find yourself resenting someone who appears to have achieved more than you.
2. You find yourself resenting someone who appears to have achieved less than you.
3. You find yourself believing that the more you give, the less you have.
4. You find yourself no longer able to see things through the eyes of your customer.
5. You find yourself in a group able/willing to justify cruelty in any form—towards customers or colleagues.

There is an old Burt Bacharach song with the lyric: "Knowing when to leave may be the smartest thing than anyone can learn." Any of the items on the list above are signals that **it's time to leave**. It is always better to make that choice before that choice is made for you, believe me.

Pay even closer attention to the things falling into place in your experience. There is something I call "the incidence of coincidence," which I always consider a sign that my mind and environment are in sync: You think of someone—they call; you think of a song—it plays on the radio; an answer to a question you've been considering falls into your lap; or you find yourself "in the right place at the right time"—these are all indicators of being tuned in to your intention. Find comfort in these cosmic winks; you're on the right track!

TAKING MY OWN ADVICE

As I come to the end of writing this book, perhaps I should take my own advice and consider the tangential effects it may have on someone who reads it. I've asked you to be brave enough to reflect on the emotional outcomes of your efforts on others, but that should work both ways. I would love to think that someone out there will animate their own dreams through service because of this book.

To be honest, at first, I started to write a book because, well, that's what speakers and consultants are supposed to do. It felt like writing a really long term-paper I had to complete to pass a class. Then something happened that I should have anticipated; as I rethought my experiences, I relived them and relearned the lessons by doing exactly what I've asked you to do—remembering.

We learn what we teach. Making the commitment to teach these ideas in a new way has allowed me to learn them in a new way. Communicating the ideas mentioned in these pages has served to solidify my own "service superpowers." You see? Serving really does serve the server first.

The more you teach this, the more you'll learn it.

> "A good teacher must believe in the ideas he teaches,
> but he must meet another condition; he must believe in the
> students to whom he offers the ideas."
> —*A Course in Miracles*

ACKNOWLEDGMENTS

Many thanks to the people who have encouraged me and continue to support my efforts in life and the speaking industry: Burt Dubin, my first mentor in speaking, Richard & Angela Schelp, Stephen Kirkpatrick, Joy Cowan, and the entire team at Executive Speakers Bureau for helping to reinvent my career—I owe you all so much. Had it not been for Gary Izzo and Ron Rodriquez I would have never had my Disney adventure in Florida, while Mark Renfro and Michael Korkis made sure it continued. I will always be indebted to Steve Riley for bringing me into "Traditions" and making me a trainer at Disney. Dennis Snow continues to inspire me as a professional speaker and human being. Thanks to "Nurse" Nancy Wilson for helping me edit as we went. It would be impossible to overstate how the talents of James Cheney upgraded my professional life with a masterful demo reel. I'm indebted to my mom, Diane Gravance, for obvious reasons and to my husband, John Graham, for loving (taking care of) me for forty years. Thank you, also, to Tony Whitten for developing the back cover art.

ABOUT THE AUTHOR

Louie Gravance is often referred to as "the guy that can make the Disney service concepts actually work outside of Disney." For over twenty-five years at the Walt Disney Company, Louie enjoyed a distinguished career with Disney theme parks, designing everything from live-entertainment experiences to customer service training programs through the Disney Institute in Orlando, Florida.

At only twelve years old, he began working in California as a stage, film, and television actor and would go on to appear in movies, sitcoms, and over thirty-five national television commercials. In 1987, Gravance was offered a summer job with one of the entertainment industry's most successful providers of "magical" customer experiences, Disney theme parks, beginning as a comic at Disneyland in Anaheim, California and soon thereafter embarking on a nearly three-decade adventure at the Walt Disney World Resort in Orlando, Florida.

Following his hugely effective tenure in Orlando, Gravance left Disney to pursue other opportunities and soon amassed even more success working as a consultant, customer service speaker, and corporate culture guru. Louie has designed multimillion-dollar service campaigns for companies such as Bank of America, ING Financial, Choice Hotels, Nikon, and The American Council of Independent Laboratories.

Gravance is the recipient of the Disney Partners in Excellence Award and the Spirit of Disney Award and has been recognized internationally as a leading keynote speaker on the topic of customer service and employee engagement.